DICTIONARY OF NUTRITION

and Food Values
by Beryl Frank

Galahad Books • New York City

Library of Congress Catalog Number: 80-85211
ISBN: 0-88365-488-1

To my editors, who love to eat —
and as always, to Lou.

CONTENTS

ONE

HOW FOOD AFFECTS HEALTH

What do a 200-pound man, a 100-pound lady, and a 10-pound baby have in common? They all have to eat. Yes, all animals, man included, use food as the fuel for their bodies. Even the unborn embryo needs proper nutrition to grow. The food we eat is converted into energy, and it is this energy which allows the body to function.

We're aware of this need for energy in such obvious ways as climbing stairs, running a race, or playing a hot game of tennis; and even in such mundane things as shopping for the food we need to create that energy. We are constantly being bombarded with reminders that we should eat a better breakfast to get a good start for the day. Proper diet is stressed in all media by such impressive national organizations as the American Medical Association, the American Heart Association, and Weight Watchers, Inc., as well as by the manufacturers of those family-oriented crunchie-wunchies which supply 100% of daily nutrient needs in every spoonful.

What does it all mean? Why does a 10-year-old student

in elementary school have different food requirements than his teenage, blue-jean clad sibling? Why can a farmer who works in his fields eat larger amounts of food than his city cousin who sits at a desk all day? Why does the same meal of meat and potatoes, topped off with a generous piece of apple pie, add unwanted pounds to one person while it in no way changes another's physique?

The answers to these questions are all found when you learn more about the food you eat. Food does affect your health. Your own eating habits can help you to live a fuller and happier life.

Many people do not begin to consider how food affects their health until, for one reason or another, they are programmed to change their eating habits by the family doctor. The problem may be as small as a little bit of overweight or a few pounds of underweight, or it may be as severe as a sudden heart attack or a case of diabetes. Each of these conditions may call for changes, either minor or drastic, in the individual's eating patterns.

But the best time to consider how food affects you is before there is an emergency of any kind. Ideally, every mother who plans family meals has an opportunity to give her family, from infancy on up, a balanced diet which will provide them with what they need to live a healthy productive life. This is not to say that the burden of good nutrition belongs solely to the meal planner. Each individual owes it to himself to understand what makes for good healthful eating.

There is no intention in this book to eliminate from the diet such delectables as a fudge sundae topped with whipped cream and a red cherry. Many people can indulge themselves this way and thoroughly enjoy it. But, before you include such a treat in your daily diet, find out if you actually benefit from this kind of eating.

There is no one magic food which can provide all of the nutrients we need. Since the complex human body requires carbohydrates, proteins, fats, vitamins, minerals, and water, a balanced diet must include a variety of foods. A piece of beefsteak may provide the needed protein. A glass of milk may provide the needed minerals. But you will lack vitamins on a meat and milk diet, unless you include some fruit or vegetables, too. Ultimately, the most sensible diet, and the one which will keep you the healthiest, is a mixture of plant and animal products.

All too often, we fail to consider how food affects our health until we are ill. The time to learn and create good, sensible eating habits is before that crisis arises. Find out whether or not a potato is a starch and falls into the carbohydrate class. Will that potato add too many unwanted calories—what is a *calorie*—or, is it the added butter or sour cream on the potato which will create excess fat? What is *cholesterol?* How much salt should be used? Are peas a better vegetable than celery?

The answers to these questions, and many more like them, are indeed the answers to how the foods you eat affect your health. You should know what is in a tomato; so that, when you eat that tomato, you are also aware of how it helps you. Everybody is affected by the food he eats, from the acne-marked teenager who should cut back on pizza and potato chips, to the late-night heavy snacker who should substitute an orange for that piece of coconut cake.

Since people are first and foremost individuals, and individual needs may vary, the person who cares about his personal nutrition should learn about the food he eats. Hopefully, that person will read on and find some of his answers here.

TWO

WHAT IS A DIET?

"My diet is the bane of my existence. I'm starving to death and still not losing weight."

"I have to force myself to eat nuts and candy bars. I must gain weight."

"I'm a diabetic and I can't have sugar in my diet."

"My cholesterol content is high, but everything good to eat is high in cholesterol."

How many times have you sat at a lunch or dinner table and heard comments like these?

All of these comments pertain to diet, and it seems that the entire American population is concerned with diet in one form or another. The little second-grade child, who is having a unit on nutrition in elementary school, knows that he should have ample supplies of milk, meat, vegetables, and fruit every day. The normal adult, if there really is such a norm, is aware that he or she must have certain foods to be able to perform at top speed, in work or play situations. And the older citizen, who may be retired, knows that he does not need as much food as he did when he was younger.

But what really is a *diet?*

The dictionary might say that a diet is that which a person or animal usually eats; therefore, an individual's diet would include everything he eats in the course of a given day. The breakfast cereal is part of that diet. But do not forget that the same breakfast cereal may be eaten with cream and sugar. Then, cream and sugar are also part of the daily diet.

Lunch may include a sandwich, perhaps bacon, lettuce and tomato. All three of these foods, plus the bread, are then part of the daily diet—and so is the mayonnaise or butter which is spread on the bread. That candy bar eaten at 4 o'clock is also part of the diet, as is dinner and the snack taken later. In short, everything that a person eats in a given period of time, in this case a day, is part of his diet.

But, you say, I thought a diet meant the things you were not allowed to eat.

A secondary definition of the word diet is indeed special limited food and drink which is prescribed usually for reasons of health. This is the diet which you doctor prescribes if he finds any one of many conditions which can be helped or prevented with a corrected method of eating.

The doctor prescribed diet is something that the individual should discuss with his own physician. It is safe to assert here that nobody should undertake any kind of a dietary change for any reason without first consulting his family doctor. Even if you are only trying to lose or gain a few pounds, have a physical check-up and determine the proper way to achieve your ends with your doctor.

Perhaps the most satisfactory definition of a diet is a regulated manner of living which has special reference to the foods you eat.

To better understand the word diet and all that it implies, it is necessary to consider some of the factors which influence diets. What is a good diet? What is a poor one? Since Mr. Average Person is not a doctor or a nutrition expert, what things can he observe that relate to poor dietary habits?

A number of people are what we will call *meal skippers*. There is first the child or adult who does not allow time to eat breakfast. Despite all of the media campaigns which stress a solid breakfast for the entire family, there are still people who rush out of the house with little or no food to break their overnight fast from eating. An extra 10 minutes of sleep means more to them than spending that time at the breakfast table. This is a poor diet habit. When breakfast is omitted, the day has not started off well.

A study of 3,500 high-school students, carried out in Massachusetts, showed that 11 percent of the boys and 19 percent of the girls had no breakfast. An additional 40 percent of the boys and 50 percent of the girls had a poor breakfast.

In a study in North Carolina, 13 percent of the students in the 9th grade missed a meal. This increased to 18 percent in the 10th grade and to 25 percent in the 12th grade.

Why do we make all this fuss about breakfast? In most instances, the body has been without food for 8 to 12 hours and needs fuel. You cannot run an automobile without gas. Why would you try to run your body without the fuel it needs?

Researchers have found that when breakfast is omitted, people take longer to make decisions, they are less steady, and their work output is less. The meal skipper who bypasses breakfast is cheating himself.

Perhaps you do eat a solid, sensible breakfast, and that is certainly good for you. But, if you skip your lunch through pressure of business, or because you think this is the way to cut down on calories, or for any other reason, you are still cheating yourself. The meal skipper does not keep the amount of food energy constant in the body and may then have to resort to a pick-up snack later in the day. Those snacks may give you the fast energy you are looking for, but they will not help you to keep a balanced diet on which you can function best. Snacking in place of a meal will not make up for a good overall program of diet.

The availability of food will also have an effect on your daily diet. While a mother may give her child a balanced bag lunch to take to school, she may not see to it that there is a healthy lunch for her at home. It is too easy for her to skip the meal or just to grab the leftovers she finds in the refrigerator. They may be delicious leftovers, but they may not give her the nutrients she needs every day.

Then there is the vending machine eater. Many companies have closed their cafeterias and installed vending machines. These dispense everything from sandwiches to potato chips, and some machines even supply fresh fruit. The lunch selected will depend on what is available. By choosing carefully, it is possible to get an adequate lunch, but is is more likely to end up with an accent on starches and sweets instead of a balanced diet.

Ethnic customs in the home can also influence the diet. In a Jewish home, for instance, the family will have to look to other sources than pork for their protein. In Spanish-American families, where the menu consists predominantly of beans and rice, the family will need to add a source of Vitamin C such as orange juice.

Regardless of the ethnic customs, the eating habits of the parents in a family can influence the children. If a mother detests salads of all kinds, she is going to be hard put to expect her family to enjoy them. If a father will not eat fish, he is setting a pattern which his children may very well follow. All of these things affect the eating habits of the entire household, which means they affect the diet. Remember, a diet is basically that which is consumed in a given time period.

Fad diets are another common reason for poor eating habits. The young woman who feels she is overweight should NOT try to lose that weight quickly with any of the one-food diets or with diet pills. These methods may indeed take off the weight, but many times they are dangerous for the overall physical condition. The man who has read an article about a salt-free diet should not stop using salt until he has ascertained with his own doctor that this is really what he needs.

With so much food available to most people, and so little physical activity, it is not easy to eat what is necessary to keep a good balance of nutrients and still maintain a normal weight. Many teenagers and women especially are looking for an easy way to control their weight. Fad diets seem to have a greater appeal than carefully controlling food intake and increasing exercise. Most fad diets do not have the balance of nutrients needed for good health. If the fad diet is to be followed for a long period of time or during periods of greater than average need, such as teen-age growing years or pregnancy, it can be even more harmful.

A sensible diet or a medically prescribed diet are both ways of eating which are directly tailored to your own needs. A diet is not and never should be something which you will start tomorrow and stop in a week. Proper diet is a way of life, whether this means adding vitamins, taking out sugar, or changing your own bad eating habits.

Diet, which is the food you eat, should provide for your daily nutritional needs. The best way you can understand those needs is to know about the food you eat—what it is and what it is made up of. The following chart offers you an idea of how the food you eat contributes toward your own health. Everybody needs a variety of food in his daily diet. There is no one perfect food. The human body needs a varied, healthful diet every day.

SERVING BY SERVING. . .
Foods Provide for Daily Needs

Stars on the chart below give a general idea of how servings of familiar foods contribute toward dietary needs—the more stars, the better the food as a source of the nutrient. The percentages given below the chart are based on the National Research Council's recommended dietary allowances for a young man. For some kinds of food, values are for a specific food. For others, values are for a food group; on a varied diet, which is common in this country, group values are likely to average as shown.

Kind of food	Size of serving (ready-to-eat)	Protein	Calcium	Iron	Vitamin A	B-vitamins Thiamin	B-vitamins Riboflavin	Vitamin C (ascorbic acid)	Food energy (in calories)
Milk, whole fluid . .	1 cup	*	****		*	*	**		160
Cheese, process Cheddar	1 oz.	*	***		*		*		105
Meat, poultry, fish (lean)	2 oz.	**		**	*	*	*		145
Eggs	1 la.	*		*	*		*		80
Dry beans	¾ cup	**	**	****		*			230
Peanut butter.	2 Tlb.	*		*					190
Bread, enriched	2 slices	*		*		*	*		120
Cereal, ready-to-eat	1 oz.			*		*			110
Citrus juice	½ cup					*		*****	55
Other fruit, fruit juice	½ cup			*	*			*	65
Tomatoes, tomato juice	½ cup			*	**			***	25
Dark-green and deep-yellow vegetables	½ cup		*	*	*****	*	*	****	45
Potatoes	1 md.			*		*		***	80
Other vegetables . .	½ cup			*	*			**	45
Butter, margarine	1 Tlb.				*				100
Sugar.	2 tsp.								30
Molasses	2 Tlb.		**.	****					95

Part of daily need from a serving:
***** About 50 percent or more.
**** About 40 percent.
*** About 30 percent.
** About 20 percent.
* About 10 percent.

U.S.D.A. Home and Garden Bulletin #1 Family Fare

THREE

WHAT IS A CALORIE?

Do you really care about the amount of heat needed to raise the temperature of one kilogram of water by one degree centigrade? At first glance, you might very well say you don't care. After all, what effect does raising water temperature have on you? Is that one of those mumbo-jumbo scientific facts which is carelessly thrown around in this age of scientific data? Not on your life—and if you want to understand the food you eat and how it affects you, a good place to start might be with raising the temperature of that one kilogram of water by one degree centigrade.

Of course, the scientific definition above is in reality the meaning of one word which is in common usage today. The word? *Calorie*—the amount of heat necessary to raise the temperature of one kilogram of water by one degree centigrade.

But saying the word calorie, which comes from the Latin word *calor* meaning heat, does not really explain what a calorie is or why it is important to your health. Another way of explaining a calorie is to say that it is the unit commonly used by food scientists to express the energy values of the food you eat. So, you might ask, why do I need to know this?

The human body functions on energy. This energy is the fuel which makes us perform in exactly the same way that any complex machine works. Before you run an automobile, you make sure it has gas. That is fuel for the car. Before you make coffee, you must plug in the coffee maker to the electrical outlet. The electricity is the fuel for the coffee pot. Even in your garden, you are concerned with the fuel your plants, shrubbery, and grass need, so you give them fertilizer and nutrients as their fuel for growing.

If you are concerned about the energy needed for your car, your coffee maker, and your garden, how can you not be equally as concerned about your own body? And the energy your body needs—the fuel for your physical system—comes directly from the food you eat. That food energy is measured in calories.

If the fuel for the body comes from food energy, then why doesn't a human being eat all day long? How can there be so many hours at night when no food is being consumed?

The body is a machine, running 24 hours a day. As your car does not need gas pumped into its tank all the while it is running, so you do not need food put into your body continuously. The food which you take in at meals goes through the chemical changes necessary to provide you with enough energy to function. Normal hunger pangs are the message of the body, telling a person he needs to replenish his supply of energy with more food or fuel.

What makes a hungry man eat a stalk of celery instead of a handful of cookies? Why does the undernourished person force down a handful of salted peanuts or a candy bar instead of that same piece of celery? Why do both of these people make their choice of food on the basis of how many calories the food contains?

The answer to these questions is based on each person's individual need. Everybody is different. Even identical twins have differences. So it is that no two people require exactly the same amount of food to give them the energy needed to perform best in their daily lives. The number of calories needed varies from person to person.

Counting calories is more necessary than counting sheep—or even counting money. Neither a sleepless night nor a lot of monmey can make up for an inbalance of calories in the daily diet. The fat cat may have sleepless nights and still be fat; the slim jim may be able to eat gobs and gobs of whipped cream and still not gain weight. It is the knowledge of calories and how they affect the body which can make a dietary difference.

Everything you do in any given day requires energy. Some things require more energy than others. It is harder for a person to ride a bicycle at moderate speed than it is for a person to sit in a chair and relax. The bicycling will use up about 175 calories. Sitting in the chair will only use up about 28 calories. If each of these people eat one ounce of a candy bar, he will consume about 150 calories. On that piece of candy alone, the person in the chair will have eaten more calories than he is using. The excess calories can turn to fat. The cyclist, on the other hand, is using more energy than he has consumed, and this may cause him to lose weight. While this may be an extreme example, because that one piece of candy is not all that either person eats, it does illustrate the effect of calories on the body.

Unused calories can turn to fat or overweight conditions. Lack of calories can cause underweight conditions. It is important to add here that a balance of calories with the amount of energy needed by the individual is NOT the only thing a person needs to know to enjoy good health. Understanding calories and how they work in the body is important, but there are other equally as important factors which will be considered later on in this book.

Overweight versus Obesity

Since excess weight is one of the most talked about problems facing Mr. Average Man (and Mrs. Average Woman, too), it is necessary to understand the terms *over-*

weight and *obesity*.

Overweight means an excess of 10 to 20 percent in body weight. This is the condition from which most people tend to suffer today. It is those extra few pounds that keep the waist bands from closing and tend to make us fuss at the dry cleaner for shrinking our clothes. These are the few extra pounds that prompt people to go on foolish crash diets, only to lose the pounds and gain them back again. Particularly as a person adds years, he may be inclined to add that small percentage of excess weight which he does not need and which may be injurious to his health.

When excess weight represents more than 20 percent of the desirable weight, the condition is called obesity. Whether you are technically obese or just overweight is something you should discuss with your doctor. He is aware of your own physical condition and is best qualified to ascertain the extent of your personal problem. Average charts describing what a man or woman should weigh are not generally a good guide to go by. Your weight may be the means of your own good health. Be sure to discuss this with your doctor before indulging in any kind of weight control.

Overweight or obesity occurs when a person continually, day after day, takes in more calories than his body needs for energy. The pounds of excess weight are related directly to the amount of EXTRA food he eats. You may gain 11 pounds of body fat in a year by drinking just one bottle of soft drink each day, or about 105 calories, BEYOND THE ENERGY YOUR BODY NEEDS. Some people can drink that soda and never gain a pound. Others will gain those 11 pounds over the extended time period. It is a question of the number of calories ingested versus the amount of energy expended.

The primary causes of overweight or obesity fall into three categories. They are learned, traumatic, and environmental. The first mentioned is perhaps the easiest to understand. Many of us have heard throughout our lives such comments at mealtime as these:

"Eat everything on your plate."

"If you eat your spinach, you may have a piece of cake for dessert."

"Let's go have a chocolate soda for that wonderful report card."

In themselves, there may be nothing wrong with any of these approaches. However, if you always have too much on your plate, cleaning it up may lead to obesity. Likewise, the cake you enjoyed for finishing the spinach may lead to excess pounds. Of course, using food as a bribe or reward for good behavior can do the same thing. It is not the eating that creates the overweight condition—it is eating in excess of the energy you use which does the dirty work.

The traumatic reasons for overweight or obesity can be uncontrollable factors. They are usually imbalances or injuries to some part of the body's metabolic system. These physical problems again call for a consultation with a doctor, rather than an attempt to handle the problem alone.

Environmental conditions present perhaps the most common causes of both overweight and obesity. Where food supply is short, in such countries as India, there is rarely a problem of this kind. In the United States, where rich foods are comparatively inexpensive, the problem does exist. That extra piece of pizza or those delicious french fries may be the cause of excess poundage.

Underweight

The problem of underweight has not received the same attention as the problem of overweight. But it is still one of our nutritional problems, and calories are involved. Some persons who are underweight do not eat enough food to meet the energy demands of their own bodies. Their imbalance in caloric intake is the reverse of the overweight or obese person. Their food is not supplying enough energy for the amount of energy they are putting out. These are the thin people who must increase their food intake. More calories taken in can replace what they are using. While a piece of candy can be poison for a fat person, it can be needed energy for a very thin one.

Underweight may also be the result of certain diseases

or glandular disturbances. While in a seemingly healthy person, it is probably caused by poor eating habits, it should not be glossed over. The thin person also should discuss his weight problem with his family doctor, and a sound balanced program of eating can then be adopted.

BECOMING CALORIE CONSCIOUS

There have been changes in food habits in recent years due to more and more people becoming calorie conscious. For example, the consumption of potatoes and sweet potatoes is only about half the per capita average of 50 years ago. Our grandparents enjoyed their potatoes. Today, we tend to drop them from the diet because of the number of calories they provide.

Another instance of a change in food habits caused by calorie conscious people is found in the use of nonfat dry milk. Consumption has risen gradually from none at the time of World War I to about 5 pounds per capita today. But, you say, it is not only the calories which are involved here. And you are right. Easy packaging, convenience, and lower cost are other reasons for the increase in the use of nonfat dry milk. It is also easier for manufacturers to use in commercially prepared foods. The fact that nonfat dry milk is lower in calories than the milk which comes directly from cows is certainly, however, a big plus in the general usage of the product.

Changes in income and way of life have also had an effect on the consumption of high calorie foods. The average consumption of corn meal and potatoes has fallen as incomes have risen and as people have moved from the farms. Higher incomes have permitted us to consume a greater variety of foods throughout the year. Availability of foods, due to rapid transportation and modern processing, has also made a change in our dietary habits.

The sources of our calories have changed considerably, too. Today, milk, meat, eggs and nonstarchy vegetables are providing a larger share of the total number of calories. The proportion of the total calories provided by grains and potatoes has been steadily declining. People are now more aware that the calories provided by a healthy, well-balanced meal are better than those same calories offered in a thick fudge sundae. You may love that thick fudge sundae, but it can only be enjoyed by the body when it is used for needed energy.

Should the calories you eat be considered the big bad wolf in your diet? Not at all. When you maintain a proper balance between the calories you take in and the energy your body expends, you will be enjoying healthy eating as well as healthy living.

FOUR

WHAT IS A CARBOHYDRATE?

Carbohydrates provide most of the energy a person needs to act, move, perform, work, and live.

"But," you might say here, "the chapter on calories said we need calories to act, move, perform, work, and live."

That is true, but those calories are the *measure* of energy. The carbohydrates are the energy itself. Any given food is composed of different nutrients. One average-size carrot contains 5 grams of carbohydrates. Those 5 grams produce 20 calories of energy. In order to get the energy from the carrot, it must be eaten and digested so that the carbohydrates can be broken down for use in the body.

Carbohydrates make up about half of the usual American diet and an even greater proportion of the diets of people in most other countries. It is the seeds of cereal, high in carbohydrates, which form a staple food almost everywhere. They give the highest yields of energy per unit of land cultivated. They are easy to store and transport, and, best of all, they are inexpensive.

Yes, we do get most of our energy from carbohydrates.

This is because sugars, starches and celluloses are all carbohydrates. All green plants form carbohydrates as well, but they are more important in nutrition for other reasons than as a source of energy.

Carbohydrates make our food sweet. Some of them cling to our teeth and serve as food for bacteria that cause tooth decay. Some determine what type of bacteria will grow in our intestines. The bulk in our food is mostly carbohydrate, which helps to prevent constipation. The body needs carbohydrates in order to use fat efficiently. There are indeed many reasons for the importance of carbohydrates to you as a person. They are part of what make you function in a healthy fashion.

Although carbohydrates serve in nutrition primarily as a source of energy, there is no specific requirement as to how much carbohydrate one should include in the daily diet. People as well as animals can survive quite well on diets containing little or no carbohydrates. This is because the body can make substitutions. When carbohydrates are not present, fats and proteins then become the sources of energy.

However, since carbohydrates are abundantly found in the food we grow and eat, it would be hard to imagine a world where people did not consume them. The native in the South Pacific is eating his share when he eats taro leaves, just as the Indiana school boy is when he finishes all of his spinach.

Low carbohydrate diets are sometimes suggested for the purpose of losing weight. This can work when the body uses fats and proteins directly as sources of energy and manufactures its own carbohydrates from other compounds such as amino acids. Like all diets, however, it should not be considered without your doctor's evaluation of this specific diet for you.

Many different carbohydrates are present in food. While every carbohydrate is made up of carbon, hydrogen, and oxygen, the particular chemical structure of these elements determines which of the different carbohydrates can be digested, absorbed, and used by the body. There can be very technical and scientific explanations of the carbohydrates and how they work. For the purposes here, it is enough to know what kinds of carbohydrates do indeed appear in what we eat.

Starch, which consists of glucose, is by far the most important carbohydrate which man can use efficiently. Cereal grains are rich in starch. Rice, wheat, sorghum, corn, millet, and rye contain 70 percent starch. Potatoes and other tubers and roots are also rich in starch. Beans and the seeds of many other vegetables such as peas have 40 percent of their dry matter as starch.

It can be noted from the list of foods above that many of our favorite foods are high in carbohydrates. The bread you eat is made of wheat flour, high in carbohydrate. Those delicious baked potatoes swimming in butter are high in starch. That piece of cake you enjoyed is also high in starch. These foods are some which are usually included on an overweight dieter's no-no list. Does this mean they should always be avoided? Of course not. Even the piece of cake can be enjoyed, as long as it is only one part of an overall balanced diet.

Another carbohydrate which occurs in food is sucrose. This is another name for sugar, and it is available as a highly refined and relatively pure carbohydrate. Sucrose is found naturally in many fruits and vegetables. It represents almost one-fourth of the carbohydrates eaten in the United States. While you might not want to sit down and eat spoonful after spoonful of granulated sugar, you certainly do enjoy a nice fresh piece of pineapple or a juicy orange. These are both good sources of carbohydrate, and they are better for you than the sugar.

Lactose or milk sugar makes up almost 40 percent of the solids in fresh whole milk, another excellent source of carbohydrate. It is possibly the only carbohydrate of animal origin that is of significance in nutrition.

While there are other carbohydrates, relatively few of them occur widely enough or are utilized well enough by the body to have much nutritional importance.

In addition to carbohydrates in the form of starches and

sugars, there are also the celluloses. Cellulose is the main structural material in plants. In the body, cellulose provides bulk. The strings on a stalk of celery, the casing on a slice of a peeled orange, or the inadvertantly swallowed seed are all somewhat indigestible. They are generally grouped as fiber and pass through the body unchanged.

Another carbohydrate not easily used by the body is raw starch. Raw potatoes contain raw starch which occurs in granules that are not readily broken down in the digestive tract. They must be finely ground or boiled before they can be digested.

Generally, only small amounts of these indigestible materials are present in our daily foods. The carbohydrates in the diet of most people in civilized areas are about 97 percent digestible.

All right, you say. Carbohydrates provide energy. We need them for bulk. They are important in the daily diet. What else?

There is something else about carbohydrates, because they affect food consumption indirectly as well as directly. They do this through their flavors. The sweetness of sugar makes foods more palatable. To make that piece of bread or toast taste better, we frequently put on some jelly or jam. We add sweetness to many sour foods, such as that half of grapefruit you prefer sweetened with sugar. This is how carbohydrates affect food consumption directly.

Many people prefer foods which are naturally sweetened by their own sugars. They specifically choose young peas and corn to get the sweeter flavor of the young vegetables. This sweetness does indeed make many foods taste better, particularly to young children. And, this is how carbohydrates can affect food consumption indirectly.

So far, the carbohydrate has shown itself to be a needed nutrient for the body, when the body is making the proper use of it. But there are two sides to every story, and the carbohydrate has another side worth mentioning.

When the body does not make proper use of carbohydrates, many things can occur. One of the most common conditions is diabetes. There are various symptoms of this disease, such as extreme weight loss. If you have any reason to suspect such a condition, stop reading this book and get to your own doctor. This is not a medical journal and all the knowledge of carbohydrates you may gather here will not help.

Another time that carbohydrates become the black-hatted bad men in the Western movie is when they help to develop tooth decay. Carbohydrates which are sticky, like a nice hard-to-chew caramel, or finely ground food which adheres to the teeth do indeed lead to tooth decay. Carbohydrates in solution are less damaging than those in solid form, which is why dentists frequently recommend washing the mouth out with water if a toothbrush is not at hand after eating.

Carbohydrates in the intestines serve two purposes, and this time they are the men who wear the white hats. One purpose is their effect on the bacteria and other microorganisms which grow in the intestinal tract; the other is that aforementioned bulk found in cellulose. Cellulose and related substances are not digested by the body. The bulk in our food, which helps to prevent constipation, consists mostly of these indigestible carbohydrates.

To sum it up, what is a carbohydrate? It is composed of carbon, hydrogen and oxygen. It appears in the form of sugar, starch and cellulose. It is found primarily in vegetable products and is a necessary nutrient which is and should be present in most people's regular diet.

FIVE

WHAT IS A PROTEIN?

The year was 1838. The man was a Dutch physician who gave up medicine to turn his work to chemistry. Gerrit Jan Mulder was the man, and his discovery was one which today is taken very much for granted.

Gerrit Jan Mulder, doctor turned chemist, announced in 1838 his conclusion that all living plants and animals contain a certain subtance without which life is impossible. The good doctor did not know what was in the substance—that was for later scientists to ferret out—but he was sure it was vital. He called the substance *protein,* from a Greek word meaning first place.

Scientists since that time have discovered that there are hundreds of different kinds of proteins—not just the one substance Mulder observed. They have learned much more about proteins, too. They have learned that man really cannot exist if he does not take in proteins so that they can act and interact within the human body. Life does depend on the proteins you eat.

If you want to see what a protein looks like, stand in front of your own mirror. You will see before you many different kinds of proteins because your muscles, skin, hair, eyes, and nails are all protein tissue. But there is more protein in the human body than can be seen in a mirrored reflection. The heart and lungs, the blood and lymph, the tendons and ligaments, the brain and nerves are all protein, too.

An even closer look into the body will reveal still more unseen protein. The genes which control your heredity are a particular kind of protein. The hormones that regulate the body processes are proteins. The enzymes, sometimes called the sparkplugs of chemical reactions, are also proteins. In short, proteins are indeed what Dr. Mulder recognized as the substance without which life is impossible.

A protein is composed of carbon, oxygen, and hydrogen—similar to the composition of a carbohydrate. But in addition to these three elements, and making the protein different from the carbohydrate, is the presence of nitrogen. Nitrogen is a structural part of all proteins.

Since protein is found in so many parts of the human body, doing so many different things, it stands to reason that all proteins are not alike. The difference depends on what is in the specific protein. In addition to carbon, oxygen, hydrogen, and nitrogen, some proteins contain sulphur, iron, phosphorous, or iodine. What is contained in the protein determines what that specific protein does in the human body.

Proteins are sometimes divided into two classes. A protein which is the same as it occurs in nature is called a *native* protein. A raw egg contains this kind of protein. When that raw egg is hard boiled, the heat changes the form of the egg from a liquid to a solid. The egg itself has been modified by cooking, but the protein molecule, now called a *denatured* protein, has not been changed. The protein remains the same in either form.

Proteins have to be made by living cells. They do not exist in the air, and they do not come directly from the sun. The cow grazing in the field can get protein from the plant matter on which she is grazing. The human, in turn, can get protein from the milk of the cow or directly from the meat of the animal.

Plants are the basic factory of all proteins. Even though you are told that meat and milk products are good sources of protein, and they are, it is plants which start the process. We depend on the steer to provide us with meat, the cow and the goat to supply our milk. But these animals must depend on plants for their source of life. It is a circle which begins with the plant manufacturing protein, the animal digesting it and changing it into its own protein, and the fertilizer eventually returning nutrients to the earth to begin protein manufacturing in the plant again.

The proteins we eat and digest are rearranged in the body to form the special and distinct proteins we need. There are complex chemical changes taking place in the body to fulfill those needs. The protein taken into the body must break down to its chemical units, the amino acids, before it can be used.

A simple and understandable analogy about amino acids is that they have the same relation to proteins as the letters of a word have to that word. Think about all of the words you can form from our twenty-six letter alphabet. This is a way of thinking about the many different kinds of proteins that can be made from amino acids. The amino acids in a protein determine its chemical characteristics and its nutritive value, as well as how it functions in the metabolism of the human body.

You can't talk much about proteins without understanding amino acids. They are the chemical units of which proteins are made. The protein from animal muscle, milk, and eggs is similar, though not identical, to the amino acid composition of human tissues. Thus, there is more protein value in meats, milk, and eggs for the human being. But there are proteins in fruits, vegetables, grains, and nuts, and these can be important, too. A well-balanced diet which includes part of all the major food groups will assure you of an ample supply of protein for the body needs. Only a portion of that protein needs to come from animal sources. This will be more fully discussed later in this chapter.

Next to water, protein is the most plentiful substance in the body. If all of the water were squeezed out of you, about half of your dry weight would be protein. One third of that protein is in the muscle; a fifth is in the bone and cartilage; one tenth is in the skin. There are a lot of proteins in the human body.

What the proteins do in the body can be broken down into four main functions. The first of these functions is that they build cells. Proteins are the chief tissue builders. They are the basic substance of every cell in the body. That certainly makes the proteins very important. But there is more.

Another function of proteins is to make hemoglobin, the blood protein that carries oxygen to the cells and carries carbon dioxide away from the cells. Ninety-five percent of the hemoglobin molecule is protein; the remaining 5 percent contains iron. Without this protein there would be no purified blood, and hence, no living body. Are proteins worth knowing about? You bet they are. They are life savers.

A third function of proteins in the body is that they form antibodies which fight infection. They give us the means of developing resistance and sometimes immunity to disease. Once you have had the measles, you develop an immunity to the disease. This is due to the action of your proteins. Vaccination for something like smallpox or polio works in the same way. The proteins form antibodies to fight the disease.

The last, and perhaps the least important function of proteins, is that they can supply energy. The body puts its need for energy above every other need. It will ignore the special functions of protein if no other source of energy is available. Since this creates an imbalance in the body, it is not healthy over a prolonged period of time.

By this time, you know what a protein is, what it is made of, and what it is supposed to accomplish in the human body. What you have not considered is how much protein you need. You may have seen advertisements on cereal boxes as to how many grams of proteins are in a single serving. What does this mean to you?

The protein requirement for the body depends on how fast the body is growing and how large it is. The faster the body is growing, the more protein it needs for building. The larger the body is, the more protein it needs for maintenance and repair. This means that a 6-foot, 200-pound man requires a larger portion of steak than his tiny, 5-foot, 100-pound wife. It's not that the steak was so expensive—the little woman simply needs less protein than her hefty husband.

When a woman is pregnant she has a period of rapid growth, and thus needs increased amounts of protein. During the second half of her pregnancy, when the fetus is growing rapidly, the mother will need as much as 20 grams additional protein. At this time she needs a chance to store protein, not only for the growth of the baby, but for her own tissues in preparation for milk production. Much of the success in nursing a baby depends on the mother's nutrition before the baby is born.

A child grows faster during his first year than at any other time in his life. A nursing infant gets the proteins he needs from his mother's milk. Infant foods on the market today are prepared with the baby's need of protein, and so offer a supply large enough to handle growth as well as maintenance of the child's body.

The second fastest period of growth is in adolescence. Again, an ample supply of proteins will take care of both the increased growth and the maintenance. One caution here. Proteins go toward maintenance before they work for growth. If an adolescent is not eating enough protein, or any other needed nutrient, his growth will suffer.

The total daily protein need increases steadily from birth to adolescence, and then gradually decreases to a maintenance level for adults. Only the adult who is increasing the amount of his muscle tissues—the athlete who is getting in shape, for example—needs more than the average amount of protein.

The exact amount of protein needed by the average person is figured in grams as related to his weight. Every doctor has charts which will give you this information. The recommended daily protein allowances for adults are 70 grams for the average man who weighs 154 pounds and 58 grams for the average woman who weighs 128 pounds. It is better to eat a little more than a little less of the recommended amount of protein, so that the body is certain to have enough protein for good maintenance.

To have your daily meals rank well in protein quality, only a portion of the protein needs to come from animal sources. You may prefer to take your proteins as a T-bone steak, but you don't have to. There are many combinations of foods which will supply you with the needed protein, such as cereal with milk, rice with fish, spaghetti with meat sauce, etc. Another way of gaining your needed protein is to drink a glass of milk with every meal in addition to foods of plant origin. That glass of milk with a big bowl of salad greens will still be giving you proteins. Important amounts of protein are found in meat, poultry, fish, milk, cheese, eggs, dry beans, dry peas, and nuts.

Think about the food you ate yesterday. In all probability, even without a real knowledge of the protein content of those foods, you will have eaten an ample supply of protein to maintain your body needs. You need proteins all through your life, from infancy on up. Since it is available in so many different foods, chances are you are getting what you need in your daily diet. It is important to your health and well being that you do so.

SIX

VITAMINS ARE VITAL

The name *vitamin* goes back to the year 1912. It was at that time that a man named Casimir Funk, working at the Lister Institute in London, chose the word *vitamine* for those substances which he thought of as life-giving chemical compounds. *Vita* stood for life, and *amine* for those chemical substances. The name was proven correct, and the term became popular in its present form of vitamin, dropping the final *e*. So much for the name. Now, what are vitamins?

Vitamins play a dramatic role in body processes. They take part in the release of energy from foods, promote normal growth of different kinds of tissue, and are essential to the proper functioning of nerves and muscle.

There are two kinds of vitamins: those known as fat soluble which are A, D, E, and K; and those known as water soluble which are all the B vitamins and ascorbic acid or vitamin C. All of the vitamins are important to health and well being. They each serve a role in the theatre of the human body. Like actors on a stage, some have more important roles than others, but all add to the success of the total play.

It is of course true that one source of the required vita-mins for health and well being is a small capsule which can be taken by both adults and children once a day. This is not usually necessary, however, for anyone who enjoys a well-balanced diet. Ordinarily, you can get all the vitamins you need from a well-chosen assortment of everyday foods.

Vitamin A

Vitamin A is a fat soluble vitamin which became very noted during World War II. At that time, men who were applying to the air corps used to eat lots of carrots, a good source of Vitamin A, to help their night vision. They were right. Vitamin A helps prevent night blindness and also maintains the external health of the eye.

In children, Vitamin A is needed to promote optimum growth, and to help keep the skin and inner linings of the body healthy and resistant to infection. It is also of use in the formation of tooth enamel.

The dietary sources of Vitamin A are of animal origin. Liver, milk and butterfat are all good sources. However, many vegetables and fruits, particularly the green and yellow ones, contain carotene which the body converts into Vitamin A. Carrots and spinach are both especially high in carotene, as are cantaloupe and papaya.

It is interesting to note here that when cows eat more fresh grass, as in the summer grazing, they will produce more Vitamin A in their milk. The milk is more enriched than that which they produce in winter.

Vitamin D

Vitamin D is important in building strong bones and teeth because it enables the body to use the calcium and phosphorous supplied by food. Few foods contain much Vitamin D naturally. Milk with Vitamin D added is a practi-cal source. Some Vitamin D is present in egg yolk, butter, and liver, while larger amounts occur in sardines, salmon, herring, and tuna.

There is a good reason why Vitamin D is sometimes called the sunshine vitamin. It can be formed in the body by exposing the skin to sunlight. This is a natural way of gaining Vitamin D, and perhaps a sound reason why mothers send their children outside to play in the sunshine—a sanity-saving request by the mother with a bona fide scientific reason behind it.

Dark skin tones result in less formation of Vitamin D than lighter tones. This is nature's way of protecting a beautiful native Tahitian girl or a South African tribesman from excessive quantities of Vitamin D. On the other hand, people living in the temperate zones of the world, where sunlight is limited through most of the year, must look to food or some other supplementary source for Vitamin D.

Without Vitamin D, the body can be subject to a disease known as rickets. This can be treated today with massive doses of the needed vitamin, but is still prevalent in those parts of the world where vitamins are either not known or not considered important.

Vitamin E

This vitamin has come to be associated with sterility, and it may be characterized as being essential for reproduction. There is no problem of overdosage with this vitamin, and its addition to some foods does prolong their shelf life. This, however, is more an economic than a nutritional reason for use.

Vitamin E is widely distributed in both plant and animal tissues, and people whose diets include fruits, vegetables, milk, whole-grain cereals, meats, and eggs are not apt to have a deficiency in this vitamin.

Vitamin K

Vitamin K plays an important role in the coagulation of blood. It prevents hemorrhaging and is frequently used medically, when needed, at such times as the delivery of a baby. Sources of Vitamin K are green leafy vegetables, liver, and egg yolks.

The Water Soluble B Vitamins

There are eleven substances in the Vitamin B complex now available in pure form. It will not be necessary here to discuss all of them in depth. Since this is not a medical book, it is only important to know about those vitamins which are of importance to the average individual.

Thiamin

The lack of thiamin in the diet causes a disease known as Beriberi. This illness can cause death in both children and adults, but it is controllable with proper amounts of thiamin in the diet.

The source of thiamin is high in the meat group, particularly in pork. It can also be found in cereal, milk and milk products, as well as in some vegetables. As has already been stated about other vitamins, a well-rounded diet including foods from all the groups will provide a sufficient amount of this nutrient.

Riboflavin

Children who do not have enough riboflavin in their diets often suffer from growth failure. Vision can be impaired, and certain mouth and tongue diseases may develop. The lack of riboflavin does not usually threaten life, but it is recognized as being essential. Milk is an outstanding source of riboflavin, as are some meats, particularly liver. It is also found in some vegetables.

Niacin

The lack of niacin causes pellagra, a disease controllable today by means of this member of the vitamin B complex. The disease can be cured in a relatively short time, even a few days, with massive doses of niacin. Meat is an excellent source of niacin, as are poultry and some fish.

B_6

This is a comparatively new substance in the recognized vitamin family and is necessary to protein metabolism. It is found mainly in plants, as well as bananas, whole grain cereals, and some vegetables.

B_{12}

Vitamin B_{12} is usually associated with pernicious anaemia, a once fatal disease. Today, this disease of the blood can be controlled with injections of this vitamin.

Vitamin C

Sailors and scurvy went together when Captain Cook sailed the seven seas. The British, rulers of the seas, expected to lose some men to this disease. Then, science moved on and learned that cirtus fruits prevented scurvy. The name "limey" for a British seaman came about when ships began to carry limes and other cirtus fruits to prevent the dreaded scurvy.

The best sources of Vitamin C or ascorbic acid, then as now, are oranges, lemons, limes, strawberries, and grapefruit. It can be found in green leafy vegetables as well.

Combinations of foods that provide sufficiently for the vitamins mentioned here are likely to supply enough of the other unspecified vitamins. A well-balanced diet will provide enough vitamins for an average person's daily needs.

SEVEN

MINERALS ARE A MUST

Minerals are inorganic substances required by the body to give strength and rigidity to certain body tissues and to help with numerous vital functions. We have all heard of salt; this is a common mineral known to scientists and nutritionists as sodium. We have all heard of calcium, a mineral needed for bone formation which is abundant in milk. Popeye the Sailor Man eats spinach galore! Is this because of the high iron content? Of course, that's where Popeye says he gets his muscles.

As in the case of many of the nutrients needed by the body, a generally well-balanced diet will provide most of the minerals needed.

Calcium, Phosphorous and Magnesium

Calcium is the most abundant mineral element in the body. Teamed up with phosophorous, it is largely responsible for the hardness of bones and teeth. About 99 percent of the calcium in the body is found in these two tissues.

The small amount of calcium and phosphorous in other body tissues and fluids aids in the proper functioning of the heart, muscles, and nerves, and helps the blood coagulate during bleeding. They also play an indispensible role in the body's use of food for energy.

Magnesium is closely related to both calcium and phosphorous in its location and its functions in the body.

Milk is a good source of calcium for the body, as are certain dark green leafy vegetables. A general rule of thumb for phosphorous and magnesium is that if your meals contain foods which provide enough protein and calcium, you will probably get enough of these minerals as well.

Iron

Iron is needed by the body in relatively small but vital amounts. It combines with protein to make hemoglobin, the red substance in the blood which carries oxygen from the lungs to the body cells and removes carbon dioxide from the cells. Iron also helps the cells obtain energy from food.

A deficiency of iron can cause anaemia, a disease of the blood which can be treated with extra doses of ferrous sulfate (commonly called iron) in pill form. Increased iron intake from foods can also help.

Only a few foods contain much iron. Liver is a good source. Lean meats, shellfish, dry beans, dry peas, dark green vegetables, and molasses also count as good sources.

The frequent use of foods providing important amounts of iron is encouraged for young children, preteen and teenage girls, and for women of child bearing age. These are the groups most liable to suffer a shortage of iron.

Sodium and Potassium

Both of these minerals are vital in keeping a normal balance of water between the cells and the fluids. They are also essential for the nerves to respond to stimulation, for the nerve impulses to travel to the muscles, and for the muscles to contract. All types of muscles, including the heart muscle, are influenced by sodium and potassium.

Salt is the main source of sodium in a person's diet. It is possible to eat too much salt, but the excess usually comes from salt added to food at the table rather than from the amounts found in the food itself. Foods from animal sources, including meat, fish, poultry, milk, and cheese, contain more salt than do foods from plant sources.

The intake of potassium is related to the calorie value of the diet because this mineral is so widely distributed among many different kinds of food.

There are other minerals considered essential which are not discussed here. These do help keep the body functioning in a smooth and orderly fashion, but they are usually provided in satisfactory amounts by a well-chosen variety of foods in the daily diet.

EIGHT

FATS, FIBER AND WATER — YOU NEED THEM ALL

If you enjoy broiled lamb chops, chances are you enjoy the taste of the crisp, outer fat with the meat. If you like bacon, you are definitely eating some fat. The same is true of the delicious piece of homemade bread which is dripping with butter. And this is all good, because everyone needs some fat in the diet.

Fats are concentrated sources of energy. Weight for weight, they provide more than twice as much energy, or calories, as either carbohydrates or proteins. Fats are also necessary to carry the fat soluble vitamins A, D, E, and K. We need some fat in the body; only too much is frowned upon.

Fat makes up part of the structure of cells and forms a protective cushion around vital organs. It spares protein for body building and repair by providing energy. Fat also supplies an essential fatty acid.

The body does not produce fatty acid, so it must be provided by food. It comes in many oils from plants such as corn, cottonseed, safflower, soybean, and wheat germ. These are referred to as polyunsaturated fats and are used in such things as margarine and cooking oils.

Saturated fats are usually the solid fats, and they are of animal origin. Butter and meat fats fall into this category. In choosing your daily meals, it is well to keep the total amount of fat at a moderate level and to include some foods that contain polyunsaturated fats.

Common sources of fats are butter, margarine, shortening, cooking and salad oils, cream, most cheeses, nuts, bacon, and other fatty meats. Many foods, such as whole milk, eggs, and chocolate, contain some fat naturally. Other foods such as baked goods, pastries, and desserts are made with fat and sometimes cooked in it. Even though excessive fat is not good for the body, everyone still needs some fat in the daily diet.

Cholesterol
Cholesterol is a fat-like substance made in the body and found in every cell. It is a normal constituent of blood and tissues. In addition to the cholesterol made in the body, some comes from foods of animal origin.

Medical authorities today suspect that too much cholesterol in the blood can form fatty deposits in the arteries and so increase the possibility of heart attacks and strokes. These authorities recommend a reduction of the intake of foods with high cholesterol count. In other words, a substitution of margarine, which is vegetable in origin, for butter which is animal in origin, will help to lower the cholesterol content of the body. Knowing what is present in the foods you eat can help you to plan a diet which fits your personal health needs. But before you decide to go on a cholesterol free diet, see your doctor. Only he is qualified to really tell you what you should have in the way of a special diet for your particular condition.

That Much Talked About Fiber
There is a new dietary miracle being written about to-

day. It is credited with being the cure-all for many of our 20th century diseases. It is claimed that many illnesses which take life in our country do not do so in places like Africa where a high fiber diet is normal. Yes, the new miracle is supposed to be fiber.

Dietary fiber is made up of three basic compounds—lignin, cellulose and hemi-cellulose. The first of these three balances the laxative effect of the other two. They must work together or not at all.

Dietary fiber is not the same as crude fiber. Crude fiber is that insoluble material left after boiling food with hot acid and alkali solutions. Dietary fiber should have some constituents that are dissolved in the same treatment. Where fiber content of food is reported, it is usually crude fiber, as there is not sufficient data available on dietary fiber.

Nutritionists accept the fact that some fiber is desirable in the diet. This is not new. An apple a day was reported to keep the doctor away in great grandmother's day—and many times, it certainly helped. But there are still many questions in many professional minds as to how much benefit there is in a high fiber diet.

Some of the claims made for fiber are undoubtedly true. However, since not all of these claims have been fully assessed, this book only mentions fiber to you and encourages you to look further for more information.

Water

Water is not, strictly speaking, a nutrient, but the human body can not function long without it. Water is essential for life. It ranks next to air or oxygen in importance. The body's need for water even exceeds its need for food. You can life for days or even weeks without food, but only for a few days without water.

About one-half to two-thirds of the body is made up of water. It is the medium of body fluids, secretions, and excretions. It carries food material from one part of the body to another.

Thus, water is the solvent for all products of digestion. It holds them in solution and permits them to pass through

49

the intestinal wall into the bloodstream for use throughout the body. It carries waste from the body as well.

Water also helps to regulate the body temperature by evaporation through the skin. It sustains the health of all the cells. Water is important, although you may not really care how much water is contained in any given food. After all, there is always that glass near the faucet to supply an extra bit of water on a hot day.

But it takes a regular and generous intake of water to perform all its jobs. That glass of water on a hot day is certainly one way. But beverages such as coffee, tea, juice, milk, and soup also supply needed water to the system. Foods such as vegetables, fruits, meats, and even breads and dry cereals contain some water. And water is formed when the body uses food for energy.

The charts in this book do not list the water content of food. This is not because water is unimportant. The body does need water. Rather, it is because so many foods provide water in themselves, that in a normal day's intake of food, you will be supplying your body with what it needs.

NINE

FOOD CHARTS

Explanation of Charts

1. % A percentage value in the column for a nutrient is the percentage of the U.S. Recommended Daily Dietary Allowance. A chart showing Recommended Daily Dietary Allowances is on page 250.

2. ★ A star in the column for a nutrient shows that the food contains less than 2% of the U.S. RDA of that nutrient.

3. — A dash in the column for a nutrient shows that no suitable value has been found, although there is reason to believe that a measurable amount of the nutrient may be present.

4. Wherever possible, food quantities are given in single portion sizes. However, if the manufacturer gives only total package or can size, those figures are used.

5. For package-mix products, values given are generally for the food as prepared using package instructions. If a mix is prepared using eggs and milk, for instance, the nutrients listed will include the additions.

6. Foods are listed alphabetically under major groups, wherever practical. In groups of similar foods, the USDA product is listed before any of the commercially prepared products. Raw products are listed first, then canned foods, and last the frozen product.

MILK, CHEESE, CREAM, IMITATION CREAM, RELATED PRODUCTS

MILK, CHEESE, CREAM, IMITATION CREAM, RELATED PRODUCTS

FOOD	Measure or Weight	Food Energy Cal.	Proteins Gms.	Carbo-hydrates Gms.	Fat Gms.	Choles-terol Mg.	Calcium Mg.	Iron Mg.	Sodium Mg.	Vitamin A IU.	Thiamin Mg.	Ribo-flavin Mg.	Niacin C Mg.	Vitamin C Mg.
MILK—Fluid														
Whole milk, 3.5% fat (USDA)	1 cup	160	9	12	9	288	288	.1		350	.07	.41	.2	2
Grade A, pasteurized, homogenized vitamin D milk (Meadow Gold)	1 cup	150	9	12	8	25	30%	★		4%	8%	30%	★	4%
Lowfat milk, 1% milkfat, vitamin A & D (Meadow Gold)	1 cup	100	8	11	2		30%	★		10%	6%	25%	★	4%
Lowfat milk, 2% milkfat, grade A, vitamin A & D (Viva)	1 cup	130	9	13	5	15	30%	★		10%	8%	30%	★	4%
Nonfat, skim (USDA)	1 cup	90	9	12	Trace		296	.1		10%	.09	.44	.2	2
Partly skimmed, 2% nonfat milk, solids added (USDA)	1 cup	145	10	15	5		352	.1		200	.1	.52	.2	2
Skim milk, vitamin A & D (Meadow Gold)	1 cup	90	8	11	1		30%	★		10%	6%	25%	★	4%

FOOD	Measure or Weight	Food Energy Cal.	Proteins Gms.	Carbo-hydrates Gms.	Fat Gms.	Choles-terol Mg.	Calcium Mg.	Iron Mg.	Sodium Mg.	Vitamin A IU.	Thiamin Mg.	Ribo-flavin Mg.	Niacin C Mg.	Vitamin C Mg.
Buttermilk, cultured, made from skim milk (USDA)	1 cup	90	9	12	Trace		296	.1		10%	.1	.44	.2	2
— Canned, Concentrated, Undiluted														
Condensed, sweetened (USDA)	1 cup	980	25	166	27		802	.3		1100	.24	1.16	.6	3
Evaporated, Unsweetened (USDA)	1 cup	345	18	24	20		635	.3		810	.1	.86	.5	3
— Dry, Nonfat Instant														
High-density, 7/8 cup needed for reconstitution to 1 qt. (USDA)	1 cup	375	37	54	1		1345	.6		30₁	.36	1.85	.9	7
Low-density, 1⅓ cups needed for reconstitution to 1 qt. (USDA)	1 cup	245	24	35	Trace		879	.4		20₁	.24	1.21	.6	5
CHEESE—American to Cheddar														
American, pasteurized processed (USDA)	1 oz.	105	7	1	9		198	.3		350	.01	.12	Trace	0

MILK, CHEESE, CREAM, IMITATION CREAM, RELATED PRODUCTS

FOOD	Measure or Weight	Food Energy Cal.	Proteins Gms.	Carbo-hydrates Gms.	Fat Gms.	Choles-terol Mg.	Calcium Mg.	Iron Mg.	Sodium Mg.	Vitamin A IU.	Thiamin Mg.	Ribo-flavin Mg.	Niacin C Mg.	Vitamin C Mg.
American, pasteurized processed (USDA)	1 cu. in.	65	4	Trace	5		122	.2		210	Trace	.07	Trace	0
Blue or Roquefort type, natural (USDA)	1 oz.	105	6	1	9		89	.1		350	.01	.17	.3	0
Blue or Roquefort type, natural (USDA)	1 cu. in.	65	4	Trace	5		54	.1		210	.01	.11	.2	0
Cheddar	1 oz.	115	7	1	9		213	.3		370	.01	.13	Trace	0
Cheddar	1 cu. in.	70	4	Trace	6		129	.2		230	.01	.08	Trace	0
— Cottage Cheese														
Creamed, curd pressed down (USDA)	1 cup	260	33	7	10		230	.7		420	.07	.61	.2	0
Uncreamed, curd pressed down (USDA)	1 cup	170	34	5	1		180	.8		20	.06	.56	.2	0
4% Milkfat Min. (Meadow Gold)	½ cup	120	14	4	5	15	6%	★		4%	★	10%	★	★
Skim milk (Breakstone)	4 oz.	91	18.6	.7	.5	0			48					

FOOD	Measure or Weight	Food Energy Cal.	Proteins Gms.	Carbohydrates Gms.	Fat Gms.	Cholesterol Mg.	Calcium Mg.	Iron Mg.	Sodium Mg.	Vitamin A IU.	Thiamin Mg.	Riboflavin Mg.	Niacin Mg.	Vitamin C Mg.
Stay 'N Shape Lowfat (Breakstone)	4 oz.	92	12	3.5	2	6			584					
Tangy Small Curd (Breakstone)	4 oz.	108	12.3	2.1	4	12			460					
2% Milkfat Viva Lowfat (Meadow Gold)	½ cup	100	14	4	2		6%	★		★	★	10%	★	★
— Cream Cheese														
Cream cheese (USDA)	1 cu. in.	60	1	Trace	6		10	Trace		250	Trace	.04	Trace	0
Cream cheese (USDA)	3 oz.	320	7	2	32		53	.2		1310	.02	.2	.1	0
Cream cheese (USDA)	8 oz.	850	18	5	86		141	.5		3500	.05	.54	.2	0
Cream cheese (Breakstone)	1 oz.	98	8.6	2	33.5	25			113					
Midget Farmer Cheese (Breakstone)	2 oz.	80	15	2.1	8	12			222					
Temp-Tee Whipped Cream Cheese (Breakstone)	1 oz.	98	8.6	2	33.5	25			113					

MILK, CHEESE, CREAM, IMITATION CREAM, RELATED PRODUCTS

FOOD	Measure or Weight	Food Energy Cal.	Proteins Gms.	Carbo-hydrates Gms.	Fat Gms.	Choles-terol Mg.	Calcium Mg.	Iron Mg.	Sodium Mg.	Vitamin A IU.	Thiamin Mg.	Ribo-flavin Mg.	Niacin C Mg.	Vitamin C Mg.
— Parmesan to Swiss														
Parmesan, grated (USDA)	1 cup	655	60	5	43		1893	.7		1,760	.03	1.22	.3	0
Parmesan, grated (USDA)	1 tbsp.	25	2	Trace	2		68	Trace		60	Trace	.04	Trace	0
Pot Style (Breakstone)	4 oz.	86	16.7	1.7	.5	0			460					
Ricotta (Breakstone)	2 oz.	90	10	4.5	11	16			84					
Swiss, natural (USDA)	1 oz.	105	8	1	8		262	.3		320	Trace	.11	Trace	0
Swiss, natural (USDA)	1 cu. in.	55	4	Trace	4		139	.1		170	Trace	.06	Trace	0
Swiss, pasteurized process (USDA)	1 oz.	100	8	1	8		251	.3		310	Trace	.11	Trace	0
Swiss, pasteurized process (USDA)	1 cu. in.	65	5	Trace	5		159	.2		200	Trace	.07	Trace	0
CREAM														
Half and half, cream and milk (USDA)	1 cup	325	8	11	28		261	.1		1160	.07	.39	.1	2

58

FOOD	Measure or Weight	Food Energy Cal.	Proteins Gms.	Carbo-hydrates Gms.	Fat Gms.	Choles-terol Mg.	Calcium Mg.	Iron Mg.	Sodium Mg.	Vitamin A IU.	Thiamin Mg.	Ribo-flavin Mg.	Niacin C Mg.	Vitamin C Mg.
Half and half, cream and milk (USDA)	1 tbsp.	20	1	1	2		16	Trace		70	Trace	.02	Trace	Trace
Light, coffee or table (USDA)	1 cup	505	7	10	49		245	.1		2020	.07	.36	.1	2
Light, coffee or table (USDA)	1 tbsp.	30	1	1	3		15	Trace		130	Trace	.02	Trace	Trace
Sour cream (USDA)	1 cup	485	7	10	47		235	.1		1930	.07	.35	1	2
Sour cream (USDA)	1 tbsp.	25	Trace	1	2		12	Trace		100	Trace	.02	Trace	Trace
Sour cream (Breakstone)	2 tbsp.	58	3.6	3.7	18.3	14			14					
Sour cream, imitation (Royal Danish - Beatrice Foods)	1 oz.	60	1	2	6	0	4%	★		★	★	4%	★	★
Sour dressing, cultured (Breakstone)	2 tbsp.	54	3.6	4.6	16.1				17					
Whipping cream, unwhipped—volume about double when whipped (USDA): Light cream	1 cup	715	6	9	75		203	.1		3060	.05	.29	.1	2

MILK, CHEESE, CREAM, IMITATION CREAM, RELATED PRODUCTS

FOOD	Measure or Weight	Food Energy Cal.	Proteins Gms.	Carbo-hydrates Gms.	Fat Gms.	Choles-terol Mg.	Calcium Mg.	Iron Mg.	Sodium Mg.	Vitamin A IU.	Thiamin Mg.	Ribo-flavin Mg.	Niacin C Mg.	Vitamin C Mg.
Light cream	1 tbsp.	45	Trace	1	5		13	Trace		190	Trace	.02	Trace	Trace
Heavy cream	1 cup	840	5	7	90		179	.1		3670	.05	.26	.1	2
Heavy cream	1 tbsp.	55	Trace	1	6		11	Trace		230	Trace	.02	Trace	Trace
Whipped topping, pressurized (USDA)	1 cup	155	2	6	14		67	—		570	—	.04	—	—
Whipped topping, pressurized (USDA)	1 tbsp.	10	Trace	Trace	1		3	—		30	—	Trace	—	—
IMITATION CREAM (products made with vegetable fats)														
Creamer, powdered (USDA)	1 cup	505	4	52	33		21	.6		200[2]	—	—	Trace	—
Creamer, powdered (USDA)	1 tbsp.	10	Trace	1	1		1	Trace		Trace[2]	—	—	—	—
Creamer, liquid, frozen (USDA)	1 cup	345	3	25	27		29	—		100[2]	—	0	—	—
Creamer, liquid, frozen (USDA)	1 tbsp.	20	Trace	2	2		2	—		10[2]	—	0	—	—

60

FOOD	Measure or Weight	Food Energy Cal.	Proteins Gms.	Carbo-hydrates Gms.	Fat Gms.	Choles-terol Mg.	Calcium Mg.	Iron Mg.	Sodium Mg.	Vitamin A IU.	Thiamin Mg.	Ribo-flavin Mg.	Niacin C Mg.	Vitamin C Mg.
Sour dressing, imitation sour cream made with nonfat dry milk (USDA)	1 tbsp.	20	Trace	1	2		14	Trace		Trace	Trace	Trace	Trace	Trace
Whipped topping, pressurized (USDA)	1 cup	190	1	9	17		5	—		340[2]	—	0	—	—
Whipped topping, pressurized (USDA)	1 tbsp.	10	Trace	Trace	1		Trace	—		20[2]	—	0	—	—
Whipped topping, frozen (USDA)	1 cup	230	1	15	20		5	—		560[2]	—	0	—	—
Whipped topping, frozen (USDA)	1 tbsp.	10	Trace	1	1		Trace	—		30[2]	—	0	—	—
Whipped topping mix (Dream Whip)	1 tbsp.	10	0	1	1		★	★	3	★	★	★	★	★
Whipped topping, powdered, made with whole milk (USDA)	1 cup	175	3	15	12		62	Trace		330[2]	.02	.08	.1	Trace
	1 tbsp.	10	Trace	1	1		3	Trace		20[2]	Trace	Trace	Trace	Trace
Whipped topping mix, low calorie (D-Zerta)	1 tbsp.	8	0	0	1		★	★	2	★	★	★	★	★

MILK, CHEESE, CREAM, IMITATION CREAM, RELATED PRODUCTS

FOOD	Measure or Weight	Food Energy Cal.	Proteins Gms.	Carbohydrates Gms.	Fat Gms.	Cholesterol Mg.	Calcium Mg.	Iron Mg.	Sodium Mg.	Vitamin A IU.	Thiamin Mg.	Riboflavin Mg.	Niacin Mg.	Vitamin C Mg.
Whipped topping, non-dairy Cool Whip (Birds Eye)	1 tbsp.	14	0	1	1		★	★	1	★	★	★	★	★
RELATED PRODUCTS—Cheese Dips														
Bacon & Horseradish (Breakstone)	1 oz.	55	5.7	4.3	17.7	11			204					
Blue Cheese (Breakstone)	1 oz.	60	5.3	4.5	18.5	14			207					
Cheddar Cheese (Breakstone)	1 oz.	60	7.6	5.4	18.7	15			164					
Cucumber & Onion (Breakstone)	1 oz.	50	3.6	5.6	15.5	11			167					
Imitation Ham & Spice (Breakstone)	1 oz.	50	4.6	6.4	16.3	12			164					
Jalapeno Pepper (Breakstone)	1 oz.	50	3.2	6.8	16	12			149					
Onion (Breakstone)	1 oz.	55	3.7	6.2	16.5	12			158					

FOOD	Measure or Weight	Food Energy Cal.	Proteins Gms.	Carbo-hydrates Gms.	Fat Gms.	Choles-terol Mg.	Calcium Mg.	Iron Mg.	Sodium Mg.	Vitamin A IU.	Thiamin Mg.	Ribo-flavin Mg.	Niacin Mg.	Vitamin C Mg.
Salami (Breakstone)	1 oz.	60	5.3	5.7	18	12			156					
— Eggs														
Eggs, large 24 oz. per dozen. Raw, or with nothing added (USDA): Whole without shell	1 egg	80	6	Trace	6		27	1.1		590	.05	.15	Trace	0
White of egg	1 white	15	4	Trace	Trace		3	Trace		0	Trace	.09	Trace	0
Yolk of egg	1 yolk	60	3	Trace	5		24	.9		580	.04	.07	Trace	0
Scrambled egg with milk and fat (USDA)	1 egg	110	7	1	8		51	1.1		690	.05	.18	Trace	0
Scrambled eggs and link sausage with coffee cake, frozen breakfast (Swanson)	1 complete breakfast	460	16	22	31		6%	8%	675	0	10%	80%	8%	0
— Milk Beverages														
Breakfast mix, instant chocolate, made with 8 oz. milk (Pillsbury)	1 pouch	290	14	38	9		25%	25%	260	30%	25%	25%	25%	30%

MILK, CHEESE, CREAM, IMITATION CREAM, RELATED PRODUCTS

FOOD	Measure or Weight	Food Energy Cal.	Proteins Gms.	Carbo- hydrates Gms.	Fat Gms.	Choles- terol Mg.	Calcium Mg.	Iron Mg.	Sodium Mg.	Vitamin A IU.	Thiamin Mg.	Ribo- flavin Mg.	Niacin C Mg.	Vitamin C Mg.
Breakfast mix, instant strawberry, made with 8 oz. milk (Pillsbury)	1 pouch	290	14	39	9		25%	25%	245	30%	25%	25%	25%	30%
Chocolate flavored drink made with skim milk and 2% added butterfat (USDA)	1 cup	190	8	27	6		270	.5		210	.1	.4	.3	3
Cocoa, homemade (USDA)	1 cup	245	10	27	12		295	1		400	.1	.45	.5	3
Cocoa, instant (Royal)	1 oz.	110	1.8	24	.7				120					
Malted milk beverage (USDA)	1 cup	245	11	28	10		317	.7		590	.14	.49	.2	2
Malted milk, dry powder, approx. 3 heaping teaspoons per ounce (USDA)	1 oz.	115	4	20	2		82	.6		290	.09	.15	.1	0
— Milk Desserts														
Custard, baked (USDA)	1 cup	305	14	29	15		297	1.1		930	.11	.5	.3	1

FOOD	Measure or Weight	Food Energy Cal.	Proteins Gms.	Carbo-hydrates Gms.	Fat Gms.	Choles-terol Mg.	Calcium Mg.	Iron Mg.	Sodium Mg.	Vitamin A IU.	Thiamin Mg.	Ribo-flavin Mg.	Niacin Mg.	Vitamin C Mg.
Golden Egg Custard Mix (Jello)	½ cup	170	6	24	6		20%	2%	180	4%	4%	15%	★	2%
— Ice Cream														
Regular, approx. 10% fat (USDA)	1 cup	255	6	28	14		194	.1		590	.05	.28	.1	1
Rich, approx. 16% fat (USDA)	1 cup	330	4	27	24		115	Trace		980	.03	.16	.1	1
Chocolate Eclair (Good Humor)	1 bar	290	5	33	15		8%	★		★	★	8	★	★
Chocolate flavor coated vanilla ice cream (Good Humor)	1 bar	310	5	22	22		10%	★		★	★	10	2	★
Strawberry Shortcake bar (Good Humor)	1 bar	250	4	29	13		8%	★		★	★	6	★	★
Toasted Almond bar (Good Humor)	1 bar	290	3	35	15		10%	★		★	★	★	★	★
Vanilla, artificially sweetened, diabetic (Louis Sherry)	½ cup	120	2	13	7		10%	★		4%	2%	8%	★	★

MILK, CHEESE, CREAM, IMITATION CREAM, RELATED PRODUCTS

FOOD	Measure or Weight	Food Energy Cal.	Proteins Gms.	Carbohydrates Gms.	Fat Gms.	Cholesterol Mg.	Calcium Mg.	Iron Mg.	Sodium Mg.	Vitamin A IU.	Thiamin Mg.	Riboflavin Mg.	Niacin C Mg.	Vitamin C Mg.
Whammy Stix, chocolate (Good Humor)	1 bar	160	3	12	11		6%	★		★	★	6	★	★
Whammy Stix, assorted ice flavors (Good Humor)	1 bar	50	0	13	0		★	★		★	★	★	★	★
— Ice Milk														
Hardened (USDA)	1 cup	200	6	29	7		204	.1		280	.07	.29	.1	1
Soft-serve (USDA)	1 cup	265	8	39	9		273	.2		370	.09	.39	.2	2
Sherbert (USDA)	1 cup	260	2	59	2		31	Trace		120	.02	.06	Trace	4
— Yogurt														
Made from partially skimmed milk (USDA)	8 oz.	125	8	13	4		294	.1		170	.1	.44	.2	2
Made from whole milk (USDA)	8 oz.	150	7	12	8		272	.1		340	.07	.39	.2	2
Flavored (Dannon)	8 oz.	200	12	32	3		40%	★		2%	4%	25%	★	★
Fruit (Dannon)	8 oz.	260	10	49	2		35%	★		★	2%	20%	★	★

FOOD	Measure or Weight	Food Energy Cal.	Proteins Gms.	Carbo-hydrates Gms.	Fat Gms.	Choles-terol Mg.	Calcium Mg.	Iron Mg.	Sodium Mg.	Vitamin A IU.	Thiamin Mg.	Ribo-flavin Mg.	Niacin C Mg.	Vitamin C Mg.
Parfait, black cherry (Breakstone)	8 oz.	256	4.3	19.8	1.6	10			136					
Parfait, peach (Breakstone)	8 oz.	254	4	20.9	1.5	8			128					
Parfait, strawberry (Breakstone)	8 oz.	260	4.2	22.3	1.6	9			128					
Plain (Dannon)	8 oz.	150	12	17	4		40%	★		2%	4%	30%	★	★
Stay 'N Shape, plain (Breakstone)	8 oz.	145	5	7.1	1.8	10			163					
Viva Swiss Style, plain lowfat (Meadow Gold)	8 oz.	180	12	23	4		40%	★		2%	4%	25%	★	★
Stay 'N Shape, strawberry (Breakstone)	8 oz.	245	4	20.6	1.4	8			136					
Viva Swiss Style, strawberry lowfat (Meadow Gold)	8 oz.	250	11	47	2		35%	★		★	2%	20%	★	★
Stay 'N Shape, vanilla (Breakstone)	8 oz.	205	4.6	14.8	1.6	10			150					
Soft frozen (Danny-Yo)	3½ oz.	115	4	21	1		15%	0		0	0	10%	0	0

MEAT, POULTRY, FISH AND SHELLFISH; RELATED PRODUCTS

MEAT, POULTRY, FISH AND SHELLFISH; RELATED PRODUCTS

MEAT

BEEF — Beef to Corned Beef

FOOD	Measure or Weight	Food Energy Cal.	Proteins Gms.	Carbo-hydrates Gms.	Fat Gms.	Choles-terol Mg.	Calcium Mg.	Iron Mg.	Sodium Mg.	Vitamin A IU.	Thiamin Mg.	Ribo-flavin Mg.	Niacin C Mg.	Vitamin C Mg.
Beef[3], cooked cuts, braised, simmered or pot-roasted (USDA): Lean and fat	3 oz.	245	23	0	16		10	2.9		30	.04	.18	3.5	—
Lean only	2.5 oz.	140	22	0	5		10	2.7		10	.04	.16	3.3	—
Beef, chipped or dried (USDA)	2 oz.	115	19	0	4		11	2.9		—		.18	2.2	—
Corned Beef, canned (USDA)	3 oz.	185	22	0	10		17	3.7		20	.01	.2	2.9	
Corned Beef Hash, canned (USDA)	3 oz.	155	7	9	10		11	1.7		—	.01	.08	1.8	
Corned Beef Hash Dinner (Banquet)	10 oz.	372	19.9	42.6	13.3		65	4	1752	352	.2	.14	3.07	13.1
Corned Beef Spread (Underwood)	1 oz.	55	3.8	Trace	4.3		3.97	.37	247	27.49	.003	.026	.368	4.194

— Ground Beef and Ground Beef Products

FOOD	Measure or Weight	Food Energy Cal.	Proteins Gms.	Carbo-hydrates Gms.	Fat Gms.	Choles-terol Mg.	Calcium Mg.	Iron Mg.	Sodium Mg.	Vitamin A IU.	Thiamin Mg.	Ribo-flavin Mg.	Niacin C Mg.	Vitamin C Mg.
Ground Beef, broiled (USDA): Lean	3 oz.	185	23	0	10		10	3		20	.08	.20	2.9	—
Regular	3 oz.	245	21	0	17		9	2.7		30	.07	.08	1.8	—
Chili con carne with beans, canned (USDA)	1 cup	335	19	30	15		80	4.2		150	.08	.18	3.2	—
Chile con carne with beans, canned (Swanson)	7¾ oz.	300	14	28	15		4%	15%	1100	30%	4%	6%	10%	10%
Chile con carne with beans, low sodium (Swanson)	7¾ oz.	340	15	33	16		4%	15%	65	25%	10%	10%	15%	10%
Chile with beans (Morton House)	7½ oz.	340	16	27	18		6%	20%		★	★	8%	10%	★
Chile con carne, without beans, canned (USDA)	1 cup	510	26	15	38		97	3.6		380	.05	.31	5.6	—
Chile without beans (Morton House)	7½ oz.	340	25	14	20		★	★		★	★	★	★	★

MEAT, POULTRY, FISH AND SHELLFISH; RELATED PRODUCTS

FOOD	Measure or Weight	Food Energy Cal.	Proteins Gms.	Carbo-hydrates Gms.	Fat Gms.	Choles-terol Mg.	Calcium Mg.	Iron Mg.	Sodium Mg.	Vitamin A IU.	Thiamin Mg.	Ribo-flavin Mg.	Niacin C Mg.	Vitamin C Mg.
Regular Manwich (Hunt - Wesson)	15.5 oz.	243	7.02	57.9	1.54	—	61	5.93	2753	7252	.31	.22	4.65	155.4
Sloppy Joes (Morton House)	5 oz.	240	15	19	11		★	★		★	★	★	★	★
— Meat Extenders for Ground Beef														
Chile Make A Better Burger (Lipton)	1 pattie	170	14	5	11		★	15%		2%	10%	10%	25%	★
Chili Tomato Hamburger Helper (Betty Crocker)	1/5 prep. pkg.	340	19	29	15		2%	20%		8%	20%	15%	25%	6%
Hamburger Stew Hamburger Helper (Betty Crocker)	1/5 prep. pkg.	290	18	23	14		4%	15%		6%	4%	10%	25%	8%
Hash Dinner Hamburger Helper (Betty Crocker)	1/5 prep. pkg.	310	18	25	15		2%	15%		★	4%	10%	25%	6%
Hickory Flavor Make A Better Burger (Lipton)	1 pattie	160	14	4	10		★	15%		★	6%	10%	20%	★

FOOD	Measure or Weight	Food Energy Cal.	Proteins Gms.	Carbo-hydrates Gms.	Fat Gms.	Choles-terol Mg.	Calcium Mg.	Iron Mg.	Sodium Mg.	Vitamin A IU.	Thiamin Mg.	Ribo-flavin Mg.	Niacin C Mg.	Vitamin C Mg.
Pizza Flavor Make A Better Burger (Lipton)	1 pattie	170	13	5	10		★	15%		★	8%	10%	25%	★
Rice Oriental Hamburger Helper (Betty Crocker)	1/5 prep. pkg.	320	18	30	14		★	15%		★	10%	10%	25%	★
Western Make A Better Burger (Lipton)	1 pattie	150	14	4	8		★	10%		★	4%	10%	15%	★
— Beef Heart to Beef Liver														
Heart, beef, lean, braised (USDA)	3 oz.	160	27	1	5		5	5.0		20	.21	1.04	6.5	1
Liver, beef, fried (USDA)	2 oz.	130	15	3	6		6	5.0		30280	.15	2.37	9.4	15
— Beef Meatpies or Potpies														
Beef potpie, baked 4¼ inch diam., weight before baking about 8 oz. (USDA)	1 pie	560	23	43	33		32	4.1	908	1860	.25	.27	4.5	7
Beef meatpie (Banquet)	8 oz.	409	16.3	40.9	20		27	5.2	908	749	.16	.09	1.2	1.6
Beef potpie (Morton)	8 oz.	390	12	34	21	46	2%	10%	1085	20%	10%	10%	15%	2%

MEAT, POULTRY, FISH AND SHELLFISH; RELATED PRODUCTS

FOOD	Measure or Weight	Food Energy Cal.	Proteins Gms.	Carbo- hydrates Gms.	Fat Gms.	Choles- terol Mg.	Calcium Mg.	Iron Mg.	Sodium Mg.	Vitamin A IU.	Thiamin Mg.	Ribo- flavin Mg.	Niacin C Mg.	Vitamin C Mg.
Beef meatpie (Swanson)	8 oz.	430	12	43	23		2%	15%	1125	25%	10%	8%	10%	★
— Beef Roast														
Roast, oven-cooked, no liquid added, relatively fat, such as rib (USDA):														
Lean and fat	3 oz.	375	17	0	34		8	2.2		70	.05	.13	3.1	—
Lean only	1.8 oz.	125	14	0	7		6	1.8		10	.04	.11	2.6	—
Roast, oven-cooked, no liquid added, relatively lean, such as heel of round (USDA):														
Lean and fat	3 oz.	165	25	0	7		11	3.2		10	.06	.19	4.5	—
Lean only	2.7 oz.	125	24	0	3		10	3		Trace	.06	.18	4.3	—
— Beef Steak														
Broiled, relatively fat, such as sirloin (USDA):														
Lean and fat	3 oz.	330	20	0	27		9	2.5		50	.05	.16	4	—

FOOD	Measure or Weight	Food Energy Cal.	Proteins Gms.	Carbo-hydrates Gms.	Fat Gms.	Choles-terol Mg.	Calcium Mg.	Iron Mg.	Sodium Mg.	Vitamin A IU.	Thiamin Mg.	Ribo-flavin Mg.	Niacin C Mg.	Vitamin C Mg.
Lean only	2 oz.	115	18	0	4		7	2.2		10	.05	.14	3.6	—
Broiled, relatively lean, such as round (USDA): Lean and fat	3 oz.	220	24	0	13		10	3		20	.07	.19	4.8	—
Lean only	2.4 oz.	130	21	0	4		9	2.5		10	.06	.16	4.1	—
Chopped Beef Steak, Hungry Man (Swanson)	18 oz.	730	20	70	41		6%	25%	2065	45%	20%	20%	45%	15%
Mushroom Gravy & Salisbury Steak (Morton House)	4 1/16 oz.	160	9	7	11		2%	6%		★	★	6%	10%	★
Swiss Steak "TV" Dinner (Swanson)	10 oz.	350	19	40	13	77	2%	15%	965	60%	10%	10%	20%	6%
— Beef Stew														
Beef and vegetable stew (USDA)	1 cup	210	15	15	10		28	2.8		2310	.13	.17	4.4	15
Beef stew (Morton House)	8 oz.	240	12	17	13		2%	15%		★	★	6%	15%	★
Beef stew, canned (Swanson)	7 1/2 oz.	190	13	18	7		2%	10%	965	50%	2%	6%	10%	10%

MEAT, POULTRY, FISH AND SHELLFISH; RELATED PRODUCTS

FOOD	Measure or Weight	Food Energy Cal.	Proteins Gms.	Carbo-hydrates Gms.	Fat Gms.	Choles-terol Mg.	Calcium Mg.	Iron Mg.	Sodium Mg.	Vitamin A IU.	Thiamin Mg.	Ribo-flavin Mg.	Niacin C Mg.	Vitamin C Mg.
Beef Stew Buffet Supper (Banquet)	32 oz.	700	50.9	90.9	14.5		127	8.8	5281	1164	.18	.36	8.82	2.7
Meatball stew (Morton House)	8 oz.	290	14	18	18		2%	10%		★	6%	15%	2%	★
— Frozen Beef Dinners														
Beef dinner (Banquet)	11 oz.	312	30.3	20.9	11.9		37	5.1	1925	175	.12	.25	5.62	7.5
Beef dinner (Morton)	10 oz.	290	21	20	13	65	4%	15%	840	80%	10%	15%	20%	30%
Beef "TV" Dinner (Swanson)	11½ oz.	370	31	34	12	82	4%	20%	1025	6%	10%	20%	30%	10%
Chopped Beef Dinner (Banquet)	11 oz.	443	18.1	32.8	26.5		68	3.6	1934	4505	.12	.22	4.46	7.2
Chopped Sirloin Beef "TV" Dinner (Swanson)	10 oz.	460	23	37	25	98	2%	20%	1105	80%	15%	15%	30%	15%
Gravy and Sliced Beef Buffet Supper (Banquet)	32 oz.	782	66.4	34.5	41.8		109	11.5	5381	200	.36	.73	17.45	.9
Gravy and Sliced Beef Cookin' Bag (Banquet)	5 oz.	116	14.6	4.8	4.3		14	2.7	852	68	.04	.11	2.64	.1

FOOD	Measure or Weight	Food Energy Cal.	Proteins Gms.	Carbohydrates Gms.	Fat Gms.	Cholesterol Mg.	Calcium Mg.	Iron Mg.	Sodium Mg.	Vitamin A IU.	Thiamin Mg.	Riboflavin Mg.	Niacin C Mg.	Vitamin C Mg.
Gravy & Sliced Beef (Morton House)	6¼ oz.	190	12	8	12		★	10%		★	★	6%	15%	★
Sliced Beef Country Table Dinner (Morton)	14 oz.	560	27	57	25		10%	20%	1200	60%	15%	20%	30%	35%
Meat Loaf Cookin' Bag (Banquet)	5 oz.	224	7.2	13.6	15.6	95	37	1.5	951	1808	.04	.06	1.43	1.6
Meat Loaf Country Table Dinner (Morton)	15 oz.	520	24	61	19	60	8%	25%	1620	70%	20%	20%	30%	60%
Meat Loaf Dinner (Banquet)	11 oz.	412	20.9	29	23.7		84	4.3	1991	2134	.16	.22	4.18	7.8
Meat Loaf Dinner (Morton)	11 oz.	370	23	28	18	60	6%	20%	1350	80%	20%	15%	30%	40%
Meat Loaf Man Pleaser (Banquet)	19 oz.	916	35.6	63.6	57.7		162	7.2	3649	8004	.27	.38	5.77	15.1
Meat Loaf "TV" Dinner (Swanson)	10¾ oz.	530	19	48	29		8%	20%	1310	10%	10%	15%	20%	20%
FRANKFURTERS														
Frankfurter, heated 8 per lb. pkg. (USDA)	1 frank	170	7	1	15		3	.8		—	.08	.11	1.4	—

MEAT, POULTRY, FISH AND SHELLFISH; RELATED PRODUCTS

FOOD	Measure or Weight	Food Energy Cal.	Proteins Gms.	Carbo-hydrates Gms.	Fat Gms.	Choles-terol Mg.	Calcium Mg.	Iron Mg.	Sodium Mg.	Vitamin A IU.	Thiamin Mg.	Ribo-flavin Mg.	Niacin C Mg.	Vitamin C Mg.
Beef franks (Eckrich)	1 frank	150	5	3	13		0	2%		0	0	2%	4%	10%
Beef franks (Oscar Mayer)	1 frank	140	5	1	13		0	2%		0	0	2%	4%	15%
Franks (12 oz.) (Eckrich)	1 frank	120	4	2	11		0	2%		0	2%	2%	2%	6%
Franks (16 oz.) (Eckrich)	1 frank	150	5	3	13		0	2%		0	4%	2%	4%	8%
Jumbo franks (Eckrich)	1 frank	190	6	3	17		0	2%		0	6%	4%	6%	10%
Beans and Franks Dinner (Banquet)	10¾ oz.	528	16.8	63.1	30.2		131	4	2153	1995	.31	.21	2.81	7.6
LAMB₃														
Lamb chop (USDA): Lean and fat	4 oz.	400	25	0	33		10	1.5		—	.14	.25	5.6	—
Lean only	2.6 oz.	140	21	0	6		9	1.5		—	.11	.2	4.5	—
Lamb chop, thick with bone, broiled	4.8 oz.	400	25	0	33		10	1.5		—	.14	.25	5.6	—

FOOD	Measure or Weight	Food Energy Cal.	Proteins Gms.	Carbo-hydrates Gms.	Fat Gms.	Choles-terol Mg.	Calcium Mg.	Iron Mg.	Sodium Mg.	Vitamin A IU.	Thiamin Mg.	Ribo-flavin Mg.	Niacin Mg.	Vitamin C Mg.
Leg roasted:														
Lean and fat	3 oz.	235	22	0	16		9	1.4		—	.13	.23	4.7	—
Lean only	2.5 oz.	130	20	0	5		9	1.4		—	.12	.21	4.4	—
Shoulder, roasted:														
Lean and fat	3 oz.	285	18	0	23		9	1		—	.11	.2	4	—
Lean only	2.3 oz.	130	17	0	6		8	1		—	.1	.18	3.7	—
LUNCHEON MEAT—Regular														
Bar-B-Q Loaf (Oscar Mayer)	2 slices	100	9	4	5		2%	2%		0	10%	8%	4%	10%
Bologna, 3 in. diameter by 1/8 in. (USDA)	2 slices	80	3	Trace	7		2	.5		—	.04	.06	.7	—
Bologna (Oscar Mayer)	2 slices	140	5	1	13		0	2%		0	8%	2%	4%	6%
Boiled ham, sliced (USDA)	2 oz.	135	11	0	10		6	1.6		0	.25	.09	1.5	—
Ham, chopped (Oscar Mayer)	2 slices	130	9	2	10		0	2%		0	25%	6%	10%	15%

MEAT, POULTRY, FISH AND SHELLFISH; RELATED PRODUCTS

FOOD	Measure or Weight	Food Energy Cal.	Proteins Gms.	Carbo-hydrates Gms.	Fat Gms.	Choles-terol Mg.	Calcium Mg.	Iron Mg.	Sodium Mg.	Vitamin A IU.	Thiamin Mg.	Ribo-flavin Mg.	Niacin C Mg.	Vitamin C Mg.
Ham, sliced, smoked, cooked (Oscar Mayer)	2 slices	60	8	0	3		0	0		0	20%	6%	10%	10%
Ham and cheese loaf (Oscar Mayer)	2 slices	140	10	1	11		2%	2%		0	20%	6%	8%	20%
Honey loaf (Oscar Mayer)	2 slices	80	10	2	3		0	2%		0	20%	8%	8%	10%
Liver cheese (Oscar Mayer)	2 slices	210	12	2	17		0	40%		130%	10%	90%	35%	0
Luncheon meat (Oscar Mayer)	2 slices	200	7	2	18		0	2%		0	10%	4%	6%	4%
Salami, cooked (USDA)	1 oz.	90	5	Trace	7		3	.7		—	.07	.07	1.2	—
Salami, dry type (USDA)	1 oz.	130	7	Trace	11		4	1		—	.1	.07	1.5	—
Cotto salami (Oscar Mayer)	2 slices	100	6	1	8		0	2%		0	6%	8%	6%	8%
Cotto salami, beef (Oscar Mayer)	2 slices	100	7	1	7		0	4%		0	2%	4%	8%	10%
Hard salami	3 slices	110	6	1	10		0	2%		0	10%	4%	6%	8%

FOOD	Measure or Weight	Food Energy Cal.	Proteins Gms.	Carbohydrates Gms.	Fat Gms.	Cholesterol Mg.	Calcium Mg.	Iron Mg.	Sodium Mg.	Vitamin A IU.	Thiamin Mg.	Riboflavin Mg.	Niacin C Mg.	Vitamin C Mg.
Salami for beer	2 slices	110	6	1	8		0	0		0	15%	4%	6%	20%
— Canned														
Bologna, beef (Oscar Mayer)	2 slices	140	5	1	13		0	2%		0	0	2%	4%	10%
Deviled ham (USDA)	1 tbsp.	45	2	0	4		1	.3		—	.02	.01	.2	—
Deviled ham (Wm. Underwood Co.)	1 oz.	97	3.9	Trace	9		5.95	.397	256	0	.028	.031	.737	.822
Liverwurst spread (Wm. Underwood Co.)	1 oz.	92	4.2	1.1	7.8		5.38	2.21	213	1756.8	.173	.346	1.502	1.275
Luncheon meat, spiced or unspiced (USDA)	2 oz.	165	8	1	14		5	1.2		0	.18	.12	1.6	—
Olive loaf (Oscar Mayer)	2 slices	130	7	6	9		6%	0		0	10%	8%	4%	2%
Pickle and Pimiento loaf (Oscar Mayer)	2 slices	130	7	7	8		4%	0		0	10%	8%	4%	6%
Sandwich spread (Oscar Mayer)	2 oz.	130	4	7	9		0	2%		0	6%	4%	4%	0

MEAT, POULTRY, FISH AND SHELLFISH; RELATED PRODUCTS

FOOD	Measure or Weight	Food Energy Cal.	Proteins Gms.	Carbo- hydrates Gms.	Fat Gms.	Choles- terol Mg.	Calcium Mg.	Iron Mg.	Sodium Mg.	Vitamin A IU.	Thiamin Mg.	Ribo- flavin Mg.	Niacin C Mg.	Vitamin C Mg.
PORK—Cured, Cooked														
Bacon, broiled or fried crisp, 20 slices per lb. pkg. (USDA)	2 slices	90	5	1	8		2	.5		0	.08	.05	.8	—
Bacon, cooked (Oscar Mayer)	3 slices	120	5	0	11		0	0		0	6%	2%	4%	0
Bacon, Canadian style (Oscar Mayer)	2 slices	90	12	0	4		0	0		0	25%	4%	15%	20%
Ham, light cure, lean and fat, roasted (USDA)	3 oz.	245	18	0	19		8	2.2		0	.4	.16	3.1	—
Jubilee ham slice, boneless (Oscar Mayer)	4 oz.	160	22	0	8		0	2%		0	70%	15%	20%	40%
Jubilee ham, canned (Oscar Mayer)	4 oz.	140	20	0	7		0	2%		0	50%	15%	25%	40%
Jubilee ham steaks (Oscar Mayer)	1 slice	70	11	0	3		0	2%		0	30%	8%	10%	30%
Ham dinner (Banquet)	10 oz.	369	16.8	47.7	12.2		151	2.5	1590	6555	.57	.23	3.38	57.1

FOOD	Measure or Weight	Food Energy Cal.	Proteins Gms.	Carbohydrates Gms.	Fat Gms.	Cholesterol Mg.	Calcium Mg.	Iron Mg.	Sodium Mg.	Vitamin A IU.	Thiamin Mg.	Riboflavin Mg.	Niacin C Mg.	Vitamin C Mg.
Ham dinner, frozen (Morton)	10 oz.	450	17	57	17	65	4%	20%	395	110%	30%	10%	15%	35%
Ham "TV" Dinner (Swanson)	10¼ oz.	380	19	47	13	61	4%	8%	1105	100%	30%	10%	20%	40%
— Fresh[3], Cooked														
Pork chop (USDA): Lean and fat	2.3 oz.	260	16	0	21		8	2.2		0	.63	.18	3.8	—
Lean only	1.7 oz.	130	15	0	7		7	1.9		0	.54	.16	3.3	—
Pork chop thick with bone (USDA)	3.5 oz.	260	16	0	21		8	2.2		0	.63	.18	3.8	—
Pork cuts, simmered (USDA): Lean and fat	3 oz.	320	20	0	26		8	2.5		0	.46	.21	4.1	—
Lean only	2.2 oz.	135	18	0	6		8	2.3		0	.42	.19	3.7	—
Pork roast, oven cooked, no liquid added (USDA): Lean and fat	3 oz.	310	21	0	24		9	2.7		0	.78	.22	4.7	—
Lean only	2.4 oz.	175	20	0	10		9	2.6		0	.73	.21	4.4	—

MEAT, POULTRY, FISH AND SHELLFISH; RELATED PRODUCTS

FOOD	Measure or Weight	Food Energy Cal.	Proteins Gms.	Carbo-hydrates Gms.	Fat Gms.	Choles-terol Mg.	Calcium Mg.	Iron Mg.	Sodium Mg.	Vitamin A IU.	Thiamin Mg.	Ribo-flavin Mg.	Niacin C Mg.	Vitamin C Mg.
Gravy and Sliced Pork (Morton House)	6¼ oz.	190	12	9	12		4%	8%		★	★	10%	15%	★
Loin of Pork "TV" Dinner (Swanson)	11¼ oz.	470	24	48	22	46	2%	8%	795	★	25%	10%	25%	8%
SAUSAGE														
Braunschweiger, slice 2-in. diam. by ¼ inch. (USDA)	2 slices	65	3	Trace	5		2	1.2		1310	.03	.29	1.6	—
Braunschweiger Liver Sausage (Oscar Mayer)	2 oz.	200	7	1	19		0	25%		90%	8%	50%	20%	4%
Beef Summer Sausage (Oscar Mayer)	2 slices	140	7	1	12		0	4%		0	4%	8%	8%	8%
New England Brand Sausage (Oscar Mayer)	2 slices	60	8	1	3		0	2%		0	15%	6%	6%	15%
Pork links, cooked, 16 links per lb. pkg. (USDA)	2 links	125	5	Trace	11		2	.6		0	.21	.09	1	—
Smokie Links Sausage (Oscar Mayer)	1 link	130	5	1	12		0	2%		0	8%	2%	4%	10%

FOOD	Measure or Weight	Food Energy Cal.	Proteins Gms.	Carbohydrates Gms.	Fat Gms.	Cholesterol Mg.	Calcium Mg.	Iron Mg.	Sodium Mg.	Vitamin A IU.	Thiamin Mg.	Riboflavin Mg.	Niacin C Mg.	Vitamin C Mg.
Summer Sausage (Oscar Mayer)	2 slices	150	7	1	13		0	2%		0	4%	4%	8%	15%
Vienna, canned, 7 sausages per 5 oz. can (USDA)	1 sausage	40	2	Trace	3		1	.3		—	.01	.02	.4	—
Wieners (Oscar Mayer)	1 link	140	5	1	13		0	2%		0	8%	2%	4%	15%
VEAL														
Medium fat, cooked, bone removed (USDA): Veal cutlet	3 oz.	185	23	—	9		9	2.7		—	.06	.21	4.6	—
Veal roast	3 oz.	230	23	0	14		10	2.9		—	.11	.26	6.6	—
Veal Parmagian (Banquet)	11 oz.	421	20.6	42.1	19		181	2.9	2527	7013	.19	.22	4.02	11.9
Veal Parmagian Cookin' Bag (Banquet)	5 oz.	287	15.9	19.5	16.2		136	1.6	1014	2366	.11	.17	2.83	1.7
Veal Parmigiana Dinner, Hungry Man (Swanson)	20½ oz.	910	38	70	53		25%	30%	2065	10%	20%	30%	30%	6%
Veal Parmigiana "TV" Dinner (Swanson)	12¼ oz.	520	23	47	27	99	15%	10%	1110	10%	15%	10%	30%	20%

MEAT, POULTRY, FISH AND SHELLFISH; RELATED PRODUCTS

FOOD	Measure or Weight	Food Energy Cal.	Proteins Gms.	Carbohydrates Gms.	Fat Gms.	Cholesterol Mg.	Calcium Mg.	Iron Mg.	Sodium Mg.	Vitamin A IU.	Thiamin Mg.	Riboflavin Mg.	Niacin C Mg.	Vitamin C Mg.
POULTRY														
CHICKEN														
Chicken, cooked, flesh only, broiled (USDA)	3 oz.	115	20	0	3		8	1.4		80	.05	.16	7.4	—
Chicken breast, fried, ½ breast with bone (USDA)	3.3 oz.	155	25	1	5		9	1.3		70	.04	.17	11.2	—
Chicken breast, fried, ½ breast, flesh and skin only (USDA)	2.7 oz.	155	25	1	5		9	1.3		70	.04	.17	11.2	—
Chicken drumstick, fried, with bone (USDA)	2.1 oz.	90	12	Trace	4		6	.9		50	.03	.15	2.7	—
Chicken drumstick, fried, flesh and skin only (USDA)	1.3 oz.	90	12	Trace	4		6	.9		50	.03	.15	2.7	—
Boneless chicken, canned (USDA)	3 oz.	170	18	0	10		18	1.3		200	.03	.11	3.7	3
Boned chicken with broth, canned (Swanson)	2½ oz.	110	15	1	6		★	4%	355	0	★	4%	20%	0

86

FOOD	Measure or Weight	Food Energy Cal.	Proteins Gms.	Carbo-hydrates Gms.	Fat Gms.	Choles-terol Mg.	Calcium Mg.	Iron Mg.	Sodium Mg.	Vitamin A IU.	Thiamin Mg.	Ribo-flavin Mg.	Niacin C Mg.	Vitamin C Mg.
Chicken a la King, canned (Swanson)	5¼ oz.	190	12	9	12		6%	4%	705	2%	0	6%	15%	0
Chicken & Dumplings, canned (Swanson)	7½ oz.	230	12	18	12		2%	8%	1030	10%	2%	8%	15%	0
Chicken spread, canned (Swanson)	1 oz.	70	4	2	5		4%	4%	230	0	★	2%	4%	0
Chicken spread, canned (Underwood)	1 oz.	63	4.4	1.1	4.5		5.38	.23	213	43.36	.054	.045	.794	.822
Chicken stew, canned (Swanson)	7½ oz.	180	10	18	7		2%	6%	1050	80%	2%	6%	15%	0
Boneless chicken frozen dinner (Morton)	10 oz.	260	15	22	12	50	6%	10%	1130	10%	8%	10%	30%	10%
Chicken a la King Cookin' Bag (Banquet)	5 oz.	138	13.6	10.4	4.7		61	1.7	892	166	.04	.1	1.73	1.1
Chicken croquette frozen dinner (Morton)	10.25 oz.	410	18	45	18	50	6%	20%	915	8%	20%	15%	25%	40%
Chicken & Dumplings Buffet Supper (Banquet)	32 oz.	1209	79.1	128.2	47.183		273	10.2	5190	782	.36	.64	14	8.2

MEAT, POULTRY, FISH AND SHELLFISH; RELATED PRODUCTS

FOOD	Measure or Weight	Food Energy Cal.	Proteins Gms.	Carbo-hydrates Gms.	Fat Gms.	Choles-terol Mg.	Calcium Mg.	Iron Mg.	Sodium Mg.	Vitamin A IU.	Thiamin Mg.	Ribo-flavin Mg.	Niacin Mg.	Vitamin C Mg.
Chicken 'N Dumplings Country Table Dinner (Morton)	15 oz.	580	21	83	20	90	8%	20%	1400	60%	20%	20%	35%	60%
Chicken 'N Dumplings, frozen dinner (Morton)	11 oz.	300	17	31	12	65	6%	15%	1280	80%	15%	15%	30%	30%
Chicken Man Pleaser (Banquet)	17 oz.	916	51.1	89.2	51.6		439	6.5	3562	4473	.24	.34	10.51	7.2
Chicken & Noodles Dinner (Banquet)	12 oz.	374	18.7		10.5		58	2.6	1710	3223	.20	.24	4.86	2.4
Chicken 'N Noodles, frozen dinner (Morton)	10.25 oz.	260	10	39	7	40	4%	10%	675	8%	8%	10%	15%	25%
Fried Chicken Country Table Dinner (Morton)	15 oz.	740	51	70	28	150	8%	25%	945	70%	20%	40%	80%	35%
Fried Chicken Dinner (Banquet)	11 oz.	530	27.8	48.4	25		284	4.6	2371	5107	.16	.25	7.02	21.5
Fried Chicken Dinner (Morton)	11 oz.	500	38	46	17	90	4%	15%	1300	60%	15%	25%	60%	35%

FOOD	Measure or Weight	Food Energy Cal.	Proteins Gms.	Carbohydrates Gms.	Fat Gms.	Cholesterol Mg.	Calcium Mg.	Iron Mg.	Sodium Mg.	Vitamin A IU.	Thiamin Mg.	Riboflavin Mg.	Niacin Mg.	Vitamin C Mg.
Fried Chicken "TV" Dinner (Swanson)	11½ oz.	570	28	48	29	68	6%	15%	1625	40%	10%	15%	45%	10%
Chicken potpie, baked, 4¼ inch diam., weight before baking about 8 oz. (USDA)	1 pie	535	23	42	31	68	68	3		3020	.25	.26	4.1	5
Chicken meatpie (Banquet)	8 oz.	427	15.4	39	23.2		50	3.2	999	531	.11	.11	3.41	1.8
Chicken potpie (Morton)	8 oz.	360	12	32	19	48	2%	10%	860	15%	10%	10%	20%	0
Chicken meatpie (Swanson)	8 oz.	450	14	44	25		4%	10%	1110	30%	10%	10%	20%	0
TURKEY														
Turkey, 1 slice white 4 inches long, 2 in. wide, ¼ in. thick and 2 slices dark, 2½ in. long, 1⅝ in. wide, ¼ in. thick (USDA)	3 oz.	162	26.8	0	5.2		7	1.5	111	—	.04	.15	6.5	—
Boned turkey with broth, canned (Swanson)	2½ oz.	110	17	0	5		★	4%	330	0	★	6%	25%	0

MEAT, POULTRY, FISH AND SHELLFISH; RELATED PRODUCTS

FOOD	Measure or Weight	Food Energy Cal.	Proteins Gms.	Carbo-hydrates Gms.	Fat Gms.	Choles-terol Mg.	Calcium Mg.	Iron Mg.	Sodium Mg.	Vitamin A IU.	Thiamin Mg.	Ribo-flavin Mg.	Niacin C Mg.	Vitamin C Mg.
Sliced Turkey Country Dinner (Morton)	15 oz.	640	26	82	24	85	6%	20%	1380	60%	20%	15%	35%	50%
Turkey Dinner (Banquet)	11 oz.	293	23.4	27.8	9.7		81	2.9	1797	3962	.16	.19	6.52	20.3
Turkey Dinner Humgry-Man (Swanson)	19 oz.	740	51	80	25		10%	25%	1645	20%	20%	15%	60%	40%
Turkey, frozen dinner (Morton)	11 oz.	370	23	33	16	60	4%	10%	1260	70%	10%	10%	30%	30%
Turkey Man Pleaser Dinner (Banquet)	19 oz.	620	39.3	73.8	18.9		135	4.3	3649	7417	.27	.32	9.06	13.5
Turkey Tetrazzini, frozen dinner (Morton)	11 oz.	470	16	47	24	35	15%	10%	800	60%	10%	20%	20%	35%
Turkey "TV" Dinner (Swanson)	11½ oz.	360	21	45	11	13	6%	10%	1060	60%	10%	10%	35%	30%
Turkey meatpie (Banquet)	8 oz.	415	14.5	40.6	21.6		107	2.6	1017	788	.11	.11	3.65	1.6
Turkey meatpie (Swanson)	8 oz.	450	13	40	26		4%	10%	1145	35%	10%	10%	15%	0

FOOD	Measure or Weight	Food Energy Cal.	Proteins Gms.	Carbohydrates Gms.	Fat Gms.	Cholesterol Mg.	Calcium Mg.	Iron Mg.	Sodium Mg.	Vitamin A IU.	Thiamin Mg.	Riboflavin Mg.	Niacin C Mg.	Vitamin C Mg.
Turkey potpie (Morton)	8 oz.	400	15	32	22	52	2%	8%	880	15%	10%	8%	20%	0
FISH AND SHELLFISH														
BLUEFISH														
Bluefish, baked with table fat (USDA)	3 oz.	135	22	0	4		25	.6		40	.09	.08	1.6	—
CLAMS														
Clams, raw, meat only (USDA)	3 oz.	65	11	2	1		59	5.2		90	.08	.15	1.1	8
Clams, solids and liquid, canned (USDA)	3 oz.	45	7	2	1		47	3.5		—	.01	.09	.9	—
Clams Casina (Mrs. Paul's)	2	220	11	19	11		2%	4%		0	0	6%	20%	4%
Clams Rockefeller (Mrs. Paul's)	2	260	10	19	17		2%	4%		2%	10%	6%	15%	2%
Clam sticks (Mrs. Paul's)	5	240	9	32	7		2%	14%		0	10%	10%	10%	0
Clam thins (Mrs. Paul's)	2	310	13	32	14		2%	8%		0	15%	10%	10%	0

MEAT, POULTRY, FISH AND SHELLFISH; RELATED PRODUCTS

FOOD	Measure or Weight	Food Energy Cal.	Proteins Gms.	Carbo-hydrates Gms.	Fat Gms.	Choles-terol Mg.	Calcium Mg.	Iron Mg.	Sodium Mg.	Vitamin A IU.	Thiamin Mg.	Ribo-flavin Mg.	Niacin Mg.	Vitamin C Mg.
Deviled clams (Mrs. Paul's)	1	180	8	14	10		2%	4%		0	4%	10%	10%	2%
Fried clams (Mrs. Paul's)	2½ oz.	270	9	25	16		0	4%		0	6%	4%	10%	4%
CRABS TO TUNA														
Crabmeat, canned (USDA)	3 oz.	85	15	1	2		38	.7		—	.07	.07	1.6	—
Crab miniatures (Mrs. Paul's)	3½ oz.	220	9	26	9		2%	2%		0	8%	10%	10%	0
Deviled crab (Mrs. Paul's)	1	160	8	18	7		2%	2%		0	8%	10%	8%	0
Filet of Ocean Fish "TV" Dinner (Swanson)	11½ oz.	440	27	38	20	95	10%	15%	1075	8%	15%	10%	25%	10%
Fish cake (Beach Haven)	2	220	11	20	7		2%	4%		0	15%	10%	15%	0
Fish cake (Mrs. Paul's)	2	210	10	23	8		4%	0		0	4%	6%	15%	0
Fish dinner (Banquet)	8¾ oz.	382	19.3	43.6	14.6		55	1.7	1473	2470	.3	.15	4.07	10.8

FOOD	Measure or Weight	Food Energy Cal.	Proteins Gms.	Carbo-hydrates Gms.	Fat Gms.	Choles-terol Mg.	Calcium Mg.	Iron Mg.	Sodium Mg.	Vitamin A IU.	Thiamin Mg.	Ribo-flavin Mg.	Niacin C Mg.	Vitamin C Mg.
Fish 'n' Chips "TV" Dinner (Swanson)	10¼ oz.	450	26	40	20	38	4%	10%	695	6%	15%	8%	25%	10%
Fish 'n' Chips Hungry Man Dinner (Swanson)	15¾ oz.	760	39	68	35		10%	10%	1115	25%	40%	20%	35%	★
Fish sticks, breaded, cooked, frozen, 3¾ by 1 by ½ in. stick	10 sticks	400	38	15	20		25	.9		—	.09	.16	3.6	—
Fish sticks (Mrs. Paul's)	4	150	9	16	5		2%	0		0	4%	4%	10%	0
Flounder fillets (Mrs. Paul's)	2	220	12	22	10		2%	2%		0	10%	8%	10%	0
Haddock, breaded, fried (USDA)	3 oz.	140	17	5	5		34	1		—	.03	.06	2.7	2
Haddock dinner (Banquet)	8¾ oz.	419	21.3	45.4	16.9		52	2.2		402	.42	.17	4.54	17.1
Haddock fillets (Mrs. Paul's)	2	230	14	24	9		2%	4%		0	10%	10%	20%	0
Haddock frozen dinner (Morton)	9 oz.	350	29	24	14	85	15%	15%	725	10%	15%	15%	25%	15%
Ocean Perch, breaded, fried (USDA)	3 oz.	195	16	6	11		28	1.1		—	.08	.09	1.5	—

MEAT, POULTRY, FISH AND SHELLFISH; RELATED PRODUCTS

FOOD	Measure or Weight	Food Energy Cal.	Proteins Gms.	Carbo-hydrates Gms.	Fat Gms.	Choles-terol Mg.	Calcium Mg.	Iron Mg.	Sodium Mg.	Vitamin A IU.	Thiamin Mg.	Ribo-flavin Mg.	Niacin C Mg.	Vitamin C Mg.
Ocean Perch dinner (Banquet)	8¾ oz.	434	19.1	49.8	17.6		45	1.6	1416	200	.22	.12	3.17	9.9
Oysters, raw meat only, 13-19 med. selects (USDA)	1 cup	160	20	8	4		226	13.2		740	.33	.43	6	—
Salmon, pink, canned (USDA)	3 oz.	120	17	0	5		167₄	.7		60	.03	.16	6.8	—
Salmon, pink (Del Monte)	7¾ oz.	310	43	0	13		45%	10%	1220	★	2%	20%	70%	★
Salmon, red sockeye (Del Monte)	7¾ oz.	340	45	0	17		50%	8%	1170	2%	2%	25%	60%	★
Sardines, Atlantic, canned in oil, drained solids (USDA)	3 oz.	175	20	0	9		372	2.5		190	.02	.17	4.6	—
Sardines in mustard sauce (Underwood)	1 oz.	52	4.2	.6	3.8		74.82	.57	224	51.3	.003	.037	1.134	.821
Sardines in soya bean oil (Underwood)	1 oz.	62	5.9	.1	4.3		78.79	.51	49	102.59	.003	.057	5.101	.624

FOOD	Measure or Weight	Food Energy Cal.	Proteins Gms.	Carbohydrates Gms.	Fat Gms.	Cholesterol Mg.	Calcium Mg.	Iron Mg.	Sodium Mg.	Vitamin A IU.	Thiamin Mg.	Riboflavin Mg.	Niacin Mg.	Vitamin C Mg.
Sardines in tomato sauce (Del Monte)	7½ oz.	330	36	4	18		70%	30%	825	★	2%	35%	50%	★
Sardines in tomato sauce (Underwood)	1 oz.	45	4.2	1.2	2.6		85.87	.51	113	222.47	.003	.045	1.587	.595
Scallops (Mrs. Paul's)	3½ oz.	210	12	24	8		6%	0		0	0	4%	15%	0
Shad, baked with table fat and bacon (USDA)	3 oz.	170	20	0	10		20	.5		20	.11	.22	7.3	—
Shrimp, canned, meat (USDA)	3 oz.	100	21	1	1		98	2.6		50	.01	.03	1.5	—
Shrimp, frozen dinner (Morton)	7.75 oz.	400	22	38	17	120	8%	20%	420	15%	20%	10%	25%	40%
Shrimp, fried (Mrs. Paul's)	3 oz.	170	9	17	11		2%	2%		0	8%	4%	10%	0
Shrimp "TV" dinner (Swanson)	8 oz.	360	9	47	15	138	6%	10%	1055	10%	20%	8%	15%	20%
Sole fillets (Mrs. Paul's)	2	220	12	22	10		2%	2%		0	10%	8%	10%	0
Tuna, canned in oil, drained solids (USDA)	3 oz.	170	24	0	7		7	1.6		70	.04	.1	10.1	—

MEAT, POULTRY, FISH AND SHELLFISH; RELATED PRODUCTS

FOOD	Measure or Weight	Food Energy Cal.	Proteins Gms.	Carbo- hydrates Gms.	Fat Gms.	Choles- terol Mg.	Calcium Mg.	Iron Mg.	Sodium Mg.	Vitamin A IU.	Thiamin Mg.	Ribo- flavin Mg.	Niacin Mg.	Vitamin C Mg.
Tuna, light chunk in oil (Del Monte)	6½ oz.	450	45	0	29		★	10%	930	★	★	6%	110%	★
Tuna Helper, creamy noodles 'n' tuna (Betty Crocker)	1/5 prepared pkg.	280	13	30	12		4%	10%		★	20%	10%	30%	★
Tuna Helper, creamy rice 'n' tuna (Betty Crocker)	1/5 prepared pkg.	250	11	33	8		2%	8%		★	15%	4%	30%	8%
Tuna meatpie (Banquet)	8 oz.	434	14.1	42.7	22.9		93	2.4	958	1498	.18	.16	3.63	1.6
Tuna potpie (Morton)	8 oz.	400	15	39	20	36	4%	10%	1085	6%	10%	10%	30%	6%

MATURE DRY BEANS AND PEAS, NUTS; RELATED PRODUCTS

MATURE DRY BEANS AND PEAS, NUTS; RELATED PRODUCTS

FOOD	Measure or Weight	Food Energy Cal.	Proteins Gms.	Carbo-hydrates Gms.	Fat Gms.	Choles-terol Mg.	Calcium Mg.	Iron Mg.	Sodium Mg.	Vitamin A IU.	Thiamin Mg.	Ribo-flavin Mg.	Niacin C Mg.	Vitamin C Mg.
MATURE DRY BEANS AND PEAS—Cooked, Drained														
Cowpeas or blackeye peas (USDA)	1 cup	190	13	34	1		42	3.2		20	.41	.11	1.1	Trace
Great Northern beans (USDA)	1 cup	210	14	38	1		90	4.9		0	.25	.13	1.3	0
Great Northern beans (Kounty Kist)	1 cup	180	10	32	1		10%	10%		★	6%	★	2%	2%
Lima beans (USDA)	1 cup	260	16	49	1		55	5.9		—	.25	.11	1.3	
Navy peas (USDA)	1 cup	225	15	40	1		95	5.1		0	.27	.13	1.3	0
Peas, split (USDA)	1 cup	290	20	52	1		28	4.2		100	.37	.22	2.2	—
Pea beans (B & M Baked Beans)	1 oz.	42	2	6.4	1		17.57	.99	102		.006	.023	.142	1.19
White or pea beans (Kounty Kist)	1 cup	190	10	34	1		10%	10%		★	8%	★	2%	2%

— Beans Canned with Liquids and Solids

FOOD	Measure or Weight	Food Energy Cal.	Proteins Gms.	Carbohydrates Gms.	Fat Gms.	Cholesterol Mg.	Calcium Mg.	Iron Mg.	Sodium Mg.	Vitamin A IU.	Thiamin Mg.	Riboflavin Mg.	Niacin C Mg.	Vitamin C Mg.
Barbecue beans (Campbell)	8 oz.	280	12	46	5		10%	15%	885	10%	8%	4%	6%	6%
Chili beans (Hunt's)	1 cup	234	14.4	41.7	1.68		88	4.1	1040	1004	.51	.15	.79	3.17
Home style beans (Campbell)	8 oz.	300	12	52	5		10%	15%	1045	8%	6%	4%	6%	6%
Kidney beans (Hunt's)	1 cup	237	14.2	44.5	.93		68	4.4	762	12.7	.32	.12	1.5	—
Kidney beans, dark red (Kounty Kist)	1 cup	190	10	36	1		6%	10%		★	8%	2%	2%	6%
Kidney beans, light red (Kounty Kist)	1 cup	210	10	40	1		6%	10%		★	8%	2%	2%	6%
Kidney beans, red (USDA)	1 cup	230	15	42	1		74	4.6		10	.13	.1	1.5	—
Kidney beans, red (B & M Baked Beans)	1 oz.	45	2.5	6.2	1.1		11.90	1.22	97	—	.003	.02	.397	.482
Old fashioned beans in molasses and brown sugar sauce (Campbell)	8 oz.	290	12	49	4		10%	20%	930	2%	6%	2%	4%	8%

MATURE DRY BEANS, PEAS AND NUTS; RELATED PRODUCTS

FOOD	Measure or Weight	Food Energy Cal.	Proteins Gms.	Carbo-hydrates Gms.	Fat Gms.	Choles-terol Mg.	Calcium Mg.	Iron Mg.	Sodium Mg.	Vitamin A IU.	Thiamin Mg.	Ribo-flavin Mg.	Niacin C Mg.	Vitamin C Mg.
Oven baked beans in tomato sauce (Morton House)	4 oz.	140	6	23	2		4%	15%		★	15%	4%	4%	★
Pork and beans (Hunt's)	8 oz.	289	13.9	55.2	2.5		87	5	1010	350	.42	.15	1.8	—
Pork and beans (Kounty Kist)	1 cup	250	8	42	5		10%	10%		2%	4%	4%	2%	15%
Pork & beans with tomato sauce (Campbell)	8 oz.	260	12	44	4		10%	20%	955	2%	8%	2%	10%	4%
Small red beans (Hunt's)	1 cup	220	13.7	40.7	.93		66	4.1	1220	12	.32	.12	1.37	—
White beans with frankfurters, sliced (USDA)	1 cup	365	19	32	18		94	4.8		330	.18	.15	3.3	Trace
White beans with pork and sweet sauce (USDA)	1 cup	385	16	54	12		161	5.9		—	.15	.1	1.3	—
White beans with pork and tomato suace (USDA)	1 cup	310	16	49	7		138	4.6		330	.2	.08	1.5	5

NUTS

FOOD	Measure or Weight	Food Energy Cal.	Proteins Gms.	Carbo-hydrates Gms.	Fat Gms.	Choles-terol Mg.	Calcium Mg.	Iron Mg.	Sodium Mg.	Vitamin A IU.	Thiamin Mg.	Ribo-flavin Mg.	Niacin C Mg.	Vitamin C Mg.
Almonds, shelled, whole kernels (USDA)	1 cup	850	26	28	77		332	6.7		0	.34	1.31	5	Trace
Almonds, dry roasted (Planters)	1 oz.	170	7	5	15	0	8%	6%	10	★	★	10%	4%	★
Cashew nuts, roasted (USDA)	1 cup	785	24	41	64		53	5.3		140	.6	.35	2.5	—
Cashews (Planters)	1 oz.	170	5	8	14	0	★	6%		★	4%	2%	2%	★
Cashews, dry roasted (Planters)	1 oz.	160	6	8	13	0	★	10%		★	2%	4%	★	★
Cashews, dry roasted (Skippy)	1 oz.	165	5.6	8	13.3	0	10	1.7	140	★	.06	.05	.4	★
Coconut, fresh meat only, piece approx. 2 by 2 by ½ inch. (USDA)	1 piece	155	2	4	16		6	.8		0	.02	.01	.2	1
Coconut, shredded or grated, firmly packed (USDA)	1 cup	450	5	12	46		17	2.2		0	.07	.03	.7	4

MATURE DRY BEANS, PEAS AND NUTS: RELATED PRODUCTS

FOOD	Measure or Weight	Food Energy Cal.	Proteins Gms.	Carbo-hydrates Gms.	Fat Gms.	Choles-terol Mg.	Calcium Mg.	Iron Mg.	Sodium Mg.	Vitamin A IU.	Thiamin Mg.	Ribo-flavin Mg.	Niacin C Mg.	Vitamin C Mg.
Mixed nuts, dry roasted (Planters)	1 oz.	160	6	6	14	0	2%	6%	★	★	2%	6%	8%	★
Mixed nuts, dry roasted (Skippy)	1 oz.	170	6.3	5.4	15.1	0	20	1	150	★	.05	.06	1.3	★
Mixed nuts, regular (Planters)	1 oz.	180	5	6	16	0	2%	4%	★	★	2%	2%	8%	★
Peanuts, roasted, salted, halves (USDA)	1 cup	840	37	27	72	0	107	3	—	—	.46	.19	24.7	0
Peanuts, dry roasted (Planters)	1 oz.	160	8	5	14	0	★	2%	195	★	★	2%	20%	★
Peanuts, dry roasted (Skippy)	1 oz.	165	8	4.1	14.5	0	15	.5	195	★	.02	.02	3.7	★
Peanuts, old fashioned (Planters)	1 oz.	170	7	5	15	0	★	2%	★	★	★	2%	15%	★
Peanut butter (USDA)	1 tbsp.	95	4	3	8	0	9	.3	—	—	.02	.02	2.4	0
Peanut butter, smooth (Peter Pan)	2 tbsp.	190	9	6	16	★	★	2%	★	★	2%	★	15%	★

FOOD	Measure or Weight	Food Energy Cal.	Proteins Gms.	Carbo-hydrates Gms.	Fat Gms.	Choles-terol Mg.	Calcium Mg.	Iron Mg.	Sodium Mg.	Vitamin A IU.	Thiamin Mg.	Ribo-flavin Mg.	Niacin C Mg.	Vitamin C Mg.
Peanut butter, creamy (Skippy)	1 tbsp.	95	4.7	2	8.3	0	5	.3	75	★	.01	.01	2.3	★
Peanut butter (S & W Nutradiet)	1 tbsp.	93	3	2	8	0	0	0		0	0	0	10%	0
Peanut butter, low sodium, smooth (Peter Pan)	2 tbsp.	190	9	4	16		★	2%	not more than 10 per 100 gms.	★	2%	★	15%	★
Peanut butter, super chunk (Skippy)	1 tbsp.	95	4.7	1.9	8.4	0	5	.3	65	★	.01	.01	2.2	★
Pecans, halves (USDA)	1 cup	740	10	16	77		79	2.6		140	.93	.14	1	2
Pecans, dry roasted (Planters)	1 oz.	190	3	5	19	0	2%	4%		★	6%	2%	★	★
Pistachios, dry roasted (Planters)	1 oz.	170	6	5	16	0	2%	8%		★	8%	4%	2%	★
Sunflower nuts, dry roasted (Planters)	1 oz.	160	7	5	14	0	2%	6%		★	2%	4%	10%	★
Walnuts, black or native, chopped (USDA)	1 cup	790	26	19	75		Trace	7.6		380	.28	.14	.9	—

VEGETABLES AND VEGETABLE PRODUCTS

VEGETABLES AND VEGETABLE PRODUCTS

FOOD	Measure or Weight	Food Energy Cal.	Proteins Gms.	Carbo-hydrates Gms.	Fat Gms.	Choles-terol Mg.	Calcium Mg.	Iron Mg.	Sodium Mg.	Vitamin A IU.	Thiamin Mg.	Ribo-flavin Mg.	Niacin C Mg.	Vitamin C Mg.
ASPARAGUS														
Asparagus, green, cooked, drained (USDA): Pieces 1½ to 2 in. lengths	1 cup	30	3	5	Trace		30	.9		1310	.23	.26	2	38
Spears, ½ in. diam. at base	4 spears	10	1	2	Trace		13	.4		540	.1	.11	.8	16
Asparagus, canned, solids and liquids (USDA)	1 cup	45	5	7	1		44	4.1		1240	.15	.22	2	37
Asparagus, all green (S & W Nutradiet)	½ cup	17	2	3	0		0	2%	9	10%	4%	6%	4%	35%
Asparagus, spears (Le Sueur)	1 cup	40	3	5	1		2%	2%		15%	4%	6%	6%	60%
Asparagus spears, cut (Green Giant)	1 cup	40	3	5	1		2%	2%		15%	4%	6%	6%	60%
Asparagus spears, frozen (Birds Eye)	3.3 oz.	25	3	3	0		2%	4%	2	15%	10%	8%	6%	60%

FOOD	Measure or Weight	Food Energy Cal.	Proteins Gms.	Carbo-hydrates Gms.	Fat Gms.	Choles-terol Mg.	Calcium Mg.	Iron Mg.	Sodium Mg.	Vitamin A IU.	Thiamin Mg.	Ribo-flavin Mg.	Niacin C Mg.	Vitamin C Mg.
Asparagus, cut spears in butter, frozen, boil in bag (Green Giant)	1 cup	90	3	7	6		2%	2%		25%	6%	6%	15%	50%
BEANS														
Baby butter beans, frozen (Birds Eye)	3.3 oz.	130	8	24	0		2%	6%	170	★	6%	2%	4%	8%
Green beans, cooked, drained (USDA)	1 cup	30	2	7	Trace		63	.8		680	.09	.11	.6	15
Green beans, canned, solids and liquid (USDA)	1 cup	45	2	10	Trace		81	2.9		690	.07	.1	.7	10
Green beans, cut (Del Monte)	1 cup	40	2	8	0		6%	8%	895	25%	4%	8%	2%	10%
Green beans, cut (S & W Nutradiet)	½ cup	20	1	4	0		2%	4%	1	4%	2%	2%	0	6%
Green beans, whole (Del Monte)	1 cup	35	2	6	0		6%	8%	925	25%	2%	6%	2%	10%
Green beans, whole, cut, or French style (Green Giant)	1 cup	30	2	6	0		4%	8%		10%	2%	4%	★	10%

VEGETABLES AND VEGETABLE PRODUCTS

FOOD	Measure or Weight	Food Energy Cal.	Proteins Gms.	Carbo-hydrates Gms.	Fat Gms.	Choles-terol Mg.	Calcium Mg.	Iron Mg.	Sodium Mg.	Vitamin A IU.	Thiamin Mg.	Ribo-flavin Mg.	Niacin C Mg.	Vitamin C Mg.
Green beans, Blue Lake, cut or whole, solids and liquid (Libby's)	1 cup	40	2	8	0		4%	10%		15%	2%	8%	★	10%
Green beans, Blue Lake, French style, solids and liquid (Libby's)	1 cup	35	2	8	0		4%	6%		10%	2%	6%	2%	10%
Green beans, whole, frozen (Birds Eye)	3 oz.	25	1	5	0		4%	2%	3	10%	20%	2%	4%	20%
Green beans, cut, French style, in butter sauce, frozen, boil in bag, (Green Giant)	1 cup	70	1	7	4		4%	4%		10%	2%	2%	★	15%
Green beans, mushroom sauce, onions, casserole (Green Giant)	1 cup	100	2	14	4		6%	6%		8%	2%	6%	2%	10%
Green beans, onions, bacon bits in light sauce, frozen, boil in bag (Green Giant)	1 cup	70	2	8	3		2%	4%		10%	2%	6%	★	10%

108

FOOD	Measure or Weight	Food Energy Cal.	Proteins Gms.	Carbohydrates Gms.	Fat Gms.	Cholesterol Mg.	Calcium Mg.	Iron Mg.	Sodium Mg.	Vitamin A IU.	Thiamin Mg.	Riboflavin Mg.	Niacin C Mg.	Vitamin C Mg.
Green beans, cut, in mushroom sauce, frozen, boil in bag (Green Giant)	1 cup	90	5	14	2		10%	4%		10%	4%	10%	2%	20%
Italian beans (Del Monte)	1 cup	60	3	11	0		4%	8%		15%	4%	10%	4%	40%
Italian green beans, frozen (Birds Eye)	3 oz.	30	2	6	0		2%	2%		10%	6%	6%	4%	35%
Italian green beans in tomato sauce, frozen, boil in bag (Green Giant)	1 cup	110	4	16	3		6%	10%	4	20%	4%	10%	6%	60%
Lima beans, immature seeds, cooked, drained (USDA)	1 cup	190	13	34	1		80	4.3		480	.31	.17	2.2	29
Lima beans (Del Monte)	1 cup	150	9	29	1		6%	25%	685	8%	4%	6%	6%	40%
Lima beans, solids and liquids (Libby's)	1 cup	160	10	30	1		6%	15%		4%	4%	6%	2%	30%
Lima beans, frozen (Fordhook)	3.3 oz.	100	6	18	0		2%	4%	105	4%	4%	4%	4%	35%
Baby lima beans, frozen (Birds Eye)	3.3 oz.	120	6	22	1		2%	4%	115	4%	4%	4%	4%	35%

VEGETABLES AND VEGETABLE PRODUCTS

FOOD	Measure or Weight	Food Energy Cal.	Proteins Gms.	Carbohydrates Gms.	Fat Gms.	Cholesterol Mg.	Calcium Mg.	Iron Mg.	Sodium Mg.	Vitamin A IU.	Thiamin Mg.	Riboflavin Mg.	Niacin C Mg.	Vitamin C Mg.
Baby lima beans, frozen, poly bag (Green Giant)	1 cup	150	6	28	1		4%	10%		2%	6%	4%	4%	15%
Baby lima beans in butter sauce, frozen, boil in bag (Green Giant)	1 cup	220	10	32	6		6%	8%		8%	4%	2%	2%	40%
Sprouted mung beans, cooked, drained (USDA)	1 cup	35	4	7	Trace		21	1.1		30	.11	.13	.9	.8
3 Bean Salad (Green Giant)	1 cup	220	4	45	3		4%	8%		8%	4%	4%	2%	15%
Yellow or wax beans, cooked, drained (USDA)	1 cup	30	2	6	Trace		63	.8		290	.09	.11	.6	16
Yellow or wax beans, canned, solids and liquids (USDA)	1 cup	45	2	10	1		81	2.9		140	.07	.1	.7	12
Wax beans, cut (Del Monte)	1 cup	35	1	7	0		4%	6%	665	2%	2%	6%	2%	15%
Wax beans, whole, cut, or French style (Green Giant)	1 cup	30	2	6	0		4%	6%		★	2%	4%	★	10%

FOOD	Measure or Weight	Food Energy Cal.	Proteins Gms.	Carbo-hydrates Gms.	Fat Gms.	Choles-terol Mg.	Calcium Mg.	Iron Mg.	Sodium Mg.	Vitamin A IU.	Thiamin Mg.	Ribo-flavin Mg.	Niacin C Mg.	Vitamin C Mg.
Wax beans, solids and liquid (Libby's)	1 cup	40	2	9	0		6%	4%		2%	4%	6%	2%	15%
Wax beans, cut, frozen (Birds Eye)	3 oz.	30	2	4	0		2%	4%	2	2%	4%	4%	2%	20%
BEETS TO COLLARD GREENS														
Beets, cooked, drained peeled, whole, 2 in. diam. (USDA)	2 beets	30	1	7	Trace		14	.5		20	.03	.04	.3	6
Beets, diced or sliced (USDA)	1 cup	55	2	12	Trace		24	.9		30	.05	.07	.5	10
Beets, canned, solids and liquids	1 cup	85	2	19	Trace		34	1.5		20	.02	.05	.2	7
Beets, cut, sliced or whole (Del Monte)	1 cup	70	2	15	0		2%	6%		★	2%	4%	2%	10%
Beets, Harvard, solids and liquid (Libby's)	1 cup	160	2	40	0		2%	4%		★	★	4%	★	8%
Beets, pickled, crinkle cut (Del Monte)	1 cup	150	2	36	0		2%	4%	655	★	2%	4%	4%	8%

VEGETABLES AND VEGETABLE PRODUCTS

FOOD	Measure or Weight	Food Energy Cal.	Proteins Gms.	Carbo-hydrates Gms.	Fat Gms.	Choles-terol Mg.	Calcium Mg.	Iron Mg.	Sodium Mg.	Vitamin A IU.	Thiamin Mg.	Ribo-flavin Mg.	Niacin C Mg.	Vitamin C Mg.
Beets, pickled, solids and liquids (Libby's)	1 cup	150	1	37	0		2%	4%		★	★	4	★	6%
Beets, shoestring, solids and liquid (Libby's)	1 cup	50	1	12	0		2%	8%		★	★	4%	★	8%
Beets, sliced (S & W Nutradiet)	½ cup	35	1	9	0		0	2%	40	0	0	2%	0	6%
Beets, sweet sour Harvard (Aunt Nellie's)	1 cup	210	3	51	1		2%	4%		★	★	6%	★	4%
Beet, whole rosebud (Aunt Nellie's)	1 cup	80	3	18	0		2%	4%		★	2%	6%	★	4%
Beets, whole, sliced or cut, solids and liquid, brine pack (Libby's)	1 cup	70	2	16	0		2%	6%		★	★	4%	★	8%
Beet greens, leaves and stems, cooked, drained (USDA)	1 cup	25	3	5	Trace		144	2.8		7400	.1	.22	.4	22
Broccoli, cooked, drained whole stalks, medium size (USDA)	1 stalk	45	6	8	1		158	1.4		4500	.16	.36	1.4	162

FOOD	Measure or Weight	Food Energy Cal.	Proteins Gms.	Carbo-hydrates Gms.	Fat Gms.	Choles-terol Mg.	Calcium Mg.	Iron Mg.	Sodium Mg.	Vitamin A IU.	Thiamin Mg.	Ribo-flavin Mg.	Niacin C Mg.	Vitamin C Mg.
Broccoli, stalks cut into ½ in. pieces (USDA)	1 cup	40	5	7	1		136	1.2		3880	.14	.31	1.2	140
Broccoli, chopped, yield from 10 oz. frozen pkg. (USDA)	1⅜ cup	65	7	12	1		135	1.8		6500	.15	.3	1.3	143
Broccoli, chopped, frozen (Birds Eye)	3.3 oz.	25	3	4	0		4%	2%	15	45%	4%	4%	★	90%
Broccoli, cut, poly bag (Green Giant)	1 cup	30	3	5	0		4%	2%		★	2%	2%	★	100%
Broccoli, spears, frozen (Birds Eye)	3.3 oz.	25	3	4	0		2%	2%	10	20%	4%	4%	2%	70%
Broccoli spears in butter sauce, frozen (Green Giant)	1 cup	90	3	8	5		6%	4%		30%	4%	8%	2%	100%
Broccoli spears, cut, in cheese sauce, frozen (Green Giant)	1 cup	130	9	13	5		20%	4%		50%	2%	15%	2%	100%
Broccoli amandine, frozen casserole (Green Giant)	1 cup	140	6	16	6		10%	6%		10%	6%	10%	2%	100%

VEGETABLES AND VEGETABLE PRODUCTS

FOOD	Measure or Weight	Food Energy Cal.	Proteins Gms.	Carbo-hydrates Gms.	Fat Gms.	Choles-terol Mg.	Calcium Mg.	Iron Mg.	Sodium Mg.	Vitamin A IU.	Thiamin Mg.	Ribo-flavin Mg.	Niacin C Mg.	Vitamin C Mg.
Broccoli, cauliflower, carrots, California Blend, frozen (Green Giant)	1 cup	30	2	5	0		4%	2%		50%	2%	2%	2%	70%
Brussels sprouts, 7-8 sprouts, (1¼ to 1½ in. diam.) cooked	1 cup	55	7	10	1		50	1.7		810	.12	22	1.2	135
Brussels sprouts, frozen (Birds Eye)	3.3 oz.	25	2	4	0		★	★	4	15%	6%	4%	2%	110%
Brussels sprouts in butter sauce, frozen (Green Giant)	1 cup	110	6	10	5		4%	4%		15%	6%	10%	2%	100%
Brussels sprouts, frozen, poly bag (Green Giant)	1 cup	50	4	8	0		2%	2%		10%	6%	6%	2%	100%
Brussels sprouts au gratin, casserole (Green Giant)	1 cup	160	10	17	6		15%	4%		4%	6%	10%	2%	100%
Cabbage, raw, coarsely shredded or sliced (USDA)	1 cup	15	1	4	Trace		34	.3		90	.04	.04	.2	33

FOOD	Measure or Weight	Food Energy Cal.	Proteins Gms.	Carbohydrates Gms.	Fat Gms.	Cholesterol Mg.	Calcium Mg.	Iron Mg.	Sodium Mg.	Vitamin A IU.	Thiamin Mg.	Riboflavin Mg.	Niacin C Mg.	Vitamin C Mg.
Cabbage, finely shredded or chopped, raw (USDA)	1 cup	20	1	5	Trace		44	.4		120	.05	.05	.3	42
Cabbage, finely shredded or chopped, cooked (USDA)	1 cup	30	2	6	Trace		64	.4		190	.06	.06	.4	48
Cabbage, celery or Chinese, raw cut in 1 in. pieces (USDA)	1 cup	10	1	2	Trace		32	.5		110	.04	.03	.5	19
Cabbage, spoon or pakchoy, cooked (USDA)	1 cup	25	2	4	Trace		252	1		5270	.07	.14	1.2	26
Carrots, raw, whole, 5½ by 1 in. (USDA)	1 carrot	20	1	5	Trace		18	.4		5500	.03	.03	.3	4
Carrots, raw, grated (USDA)	1 cup	45	1	11	Trace		41	.8		12100	.06	.06	.7	9
Carrots, cooked, diced (USDA)	1 cup	45	1	10	Trace		48	.9		15220	.08	.07	.7	9
Carrots, canned, diced or sliced (Del Monte)	1 cup	60	2	15	0		6%	4%	565	900%	4%	4%	6%	8%

VEGETABLES AND VEGETABLE PRODUCTS

FOOD	Measure or Weight	Food Energy Cal.	Proteins Gms.	Carbohydrates Gms.	Fat Gms.	Cholesterol Mg.	Calcium Mg.	Iron Mg.	Sodium Mg.	Vitamin A IU.	Thiamin Mg.	Riboflavin Mg.	Niacin C Mg.	Vitamin C Mg.
Carrots, canned, diced or sliced (Libby's)	1 cup	40	1	9	0		6%	2%		400%	2%	2%	2%	6%
Carrots, sliced (S & W Nutradiet)	½ cup	30	0	7	0		2%	4%	50	250%	0	0	0	2%
Carrots, crinkle cut honey glazed, frozen (Green Giant)	1 cup	170	2	30	5		6%	4%		100%	2%	6%	2%	20%
Carrot nuggets in butter sauce, frozen (Green Giant)	1 cup	100	1	12	5		4%	2%		100%	2%	2%	2%	15%
Cauliflower, cooked, flowerbuds (USDA)	1 cup	25	3	5	Trace		25	.8		70	.11	.1	.7	66
Cauliflower, frozen (Birds Eye)	3.3 oz.	25	2	4	0		★	★	10	★	4%	2%	2%	80%
Cauliflower, frozen, poly bag (Green Giant)	1 cup	25	2	4	0		2%	2%		★	★	2%	2%	60%
Cauliflower in butter sauce, frozen (Green Giant)	1 cup	80	3	6	5		2%	2%		6%	2%	6%	2%	90%

FOOD	Measure or Weight	Food Energy Cal.	Proteins Gms.	Carbohydrates Gms.	Fat Gms.	Cholesterol Mg.	Calcium Mg.	Iron Mg.	Sodium Mg.	Vitamin A IU.	Thiamin Mg.	Riboflavin Mg.	Niacin Mg.	Vitamin C Mg.
Cauliflower in cheese sauce, frozen (Green Giant)	1 cup	150	8	15	6		20%	2%		30%	4%	10%	2%	100%
Cauliflower, Hungarian frozen casserole (Green Giant)	1 cup	130	4	14	6		10%	4%		4%	2%	6%	*	90%
Celery, raw, large outer stalk, 8 by 1½ in. at root end (USDA)	1 stalk	5	Trace	2	Trace		16	.1		100	.01	.01	.1	4
Celery, raw, pieces, diced (USDA)	1 cup	15	1	4	1		39	.3		240	.03	.03	.3	9
Collards, cooked (USDA)	1 cup	55	5	9	1		289	1.1		10260	.27	.37	2.4	87
Collard greens, chopped, frozen (Birds Eye)	3.3 oz.	30	2	4	0		20%	4%	45	120%	2%	6%	2%	70%
CORN														
Corn, sweet, cooked, ear 5 by 1¾ in.[5](USDA)	1 ear	70	3	16	1		2	.5		310[6]	.09	.08	1	7
Corn, canned, solids and liquid (USDA)	1 cup	170	5	40	2		10	1		690[6]	.07	.12	2.3	13

VEGETABLES AND VEGETABLE PRODUCTS

FOOD	Measure or Weight	Food Energy Cal.	Proteins Gms.	Carbo-hydrates Gms.	Fat Gms.	Choles-terol Mg.	Calcium Mg.	Iron Mg.	Sodium Mg.	Vitamin A IU.	Thiamin Mg.	Ribo-flavin Mg.	Niacin C Mg.	Vitamin C Mg.
Corn, golden cream style (Del Monte)	1 cup	210	5	46	1		★	6%	655	6%	4%	8%	10%	25%
Corn, golden cream style (Green Giant)	1 cup	210	4	45	2		★	4%		6%	2%	4%	6%	20%
Corn, golden, family style (Del Monte)	1 cup	170	4	37	1		★	4%	635	4%	6%	8%	10%	25%
Corn, golden, vacuum packed (Del Monte)	1 cup	200	6	43	1		★	6%	465	10%	8%	10%	10%	35%
Corn, golden, whole kernel liquid pack (Green Giant)	1 cup	160	4	33	1		★	4%		6%	2%	6%	8%	20%
Corn, golden, whole kernel liquid pack (Le Sueur)	1 cup	170	4	35	1		★	4%		6%	2%	6%	6%	20%
Corn, cream style (S & W Nutradiet)	½ cup	100	3	21	1		0	4%	4	10%	0	2%	10%	12%
Corn, sweet, cream style (Libby's)	1 cup	170	4	42	2		★	4%		6%	2%	8%	10%	15%

FOOD	Measure or Weight	Food Energy Cal.	Proteins Gms.	Carbohydrates Gms.	Fat Gms.	Cholesterol Mg.	Calcium Mg.	Iron Mg.	Sodium Mg.	Vitamin A IU.	Thiamin Mg.	Riboflavin Mg.	Niacin C Mg.	Vitamin C Mg.
Corn, white cream style (Del Monte)	1 cup	190	4	42	1		★	6%	565	★	4%	10%	15%	30%
Corn, white whole kernel (Del Monte)	1 cup	150	4	33	1		★	4%	665	★	6%	8%	10%	35%
Corn, white whole kernel, vacuum pack (Green Giant)	1 cup	150	4	30	1		★	4%		★	2%	6%	6%	25%
Corn, whole kernel, wet pack (Libby's)	1 cup	160	5	37	2		★	4%		6%	4%	10%	10%	20%
Corn, whole kernel (S & W Nutradiet)	½ cup	80	2	15	1		0	6%	4	10%	0	2%	6%	8%
Corn, whole kernel, sweet, frozen (Birds Eye)	3.3 oz.	30	2	5	0		★	★	2	4%	4%	2%	6%	10%
Corn, white, whole kernel, frozen (Green Giant)	1 cup	130	4	26	1		★	2%		★	4%	4%	8%	15%
Corn, white, whole kernel in butter sauce, frozen (Mexicorn)	1 cup	190	4	30	6		★	2%		★	4%	4%	10%	15%

VEGETABLES AND VEGETABLE PRODUCTS

FOOD	Measure or Weight	Food Energy Cal.	Proteins Gms.	Carbo-hydrates Gms.	Fat Gms.	Choles-terol Mg.	Calcium Mg.	Iron Mg.	Sodium Mg.	Vitamin A IU.	Thiamin Mg.	Ribo-flavin Mg.	Niacin C Mg.	Vitamin C Mg.
Golden corn, whole kernel, frozen (Green Giant)	1 cup	130	4	26	1		*	2%		6%	4%	4%	8%	15%
Golden corn in butter sauce, frozen (Niblets)	1 cup	190	4	30	6		*	4%		10%	4%	4%	6%	15%
Corn on the cob, frozen (Birds Eye)	1 ear	130	4	28	1		*	4%	3	4%	10%	6%	10%	20%
Corn on the cob, frozen (Green Giant)	5½ in. ear	160	4	33	1		*	4%		6%	4%	6%	6%	20%
Corn on the cob, frozen (Green Giant)	3 in. coblett	90	2	18	1		*	2%		2%	2%	2%	4%	10%
Corn fritters, frozen (Mrs. Paul's)	2 fritters	260	6	31	12		0	2%		2%	2%	4%	15%	2%
Corn 'n' Peppers (Del Monte)	1 cup	190	5	40	1		*	6%	435	15%	6%	10%	10%	35%
Golden corn/peppers in butter sauce (Mexicorn)	1 cup	190	4	30	6		*	2%		10%	4%	4%	8%	20%

FOOD	Measure or Weight	Food Energy Cal.	Proteins Gms.	Carbo-hydrates Gms.	Fat Gms.	Choles-terol Mg.	Calcium Mg.	Iron Mg.	Sodium Mg.	Vitamin A IU.	Thiamin Mg.	Ribo-flavin Mg.	Niacin Mg.	Vitamin C Mg.
Scalloped corn casserole, frozen (Green Giant)	1 cup	330	9	40	15		15%	8%		6%	6%	15%	6%	10%
COWPEAS TO PARSNIPS														
Cowpeas, cooked, immature seeds (USDA)	1 cup	175	13	29	1		38	3.4		560	.49	.18	2.3	28
Cucumbers, 10 oz., 7½ by about 2 in., raw, pared (USDA)	1 cucumber	30	1	7	Trace		35	.6		Trace	.07	.09	.4	23
Dandelion greens, cooked (USDA)	1 cup	60	4	12	1		252	3.2		21060	.24	.29	—	32
Eggplant, cooked, boiled, drained, diced (USDA)	1 cup	38	2	8.2	.4		22	1.2		20	.1	.08	1	6
Eggplant parmesan, frozen (Mrs. Paul's)	5½ oz.	250	8	21	16		6%	2%		15%	2%	8%	4%	2%
Eggplant slices, frozen (Mrs. Paul's)	3 oz.	230	4	22	15		0	4%		0	2%	0	10%	0
Eggplant sticks, frozen (Mrs. Paul's)	3½ oz.	260	5	27	15		0	4%		0	4%	2%	6%	2%

VEGETABLES AND VEGETABLE PRODUCTS

FOOD	Measure or Weight	Food Energy Cal.	Proteins Gms.	Carbo-hydrates Gms.	Fat Gms.	Choles-terol Mg.	Calcium Mg.	Iron Mg.	Sodium Mg.	Vitamin A IU.	Thiamin Mg.	Ribo-flavin Mg.	Niacin C Mg.	Vitamin C Mg.
Endive, curly, including escarole (USDA)	2 oz.	10	1	2	Trace		46	1		1870	.04	.08	.3	6
Kale, leaves, including stems, cooked (USDA)	1 cup	30	4	4	1		147	1.3		8140	—	—	—	68
Lettuce, Boston types, head 4 in. diameter (USDA)	1 head	30	3	6	Trace		77	4.4	.23	2130	.14	.13	.6	18
Lettuce, crisp, Iceberg, 4¾ in. diameter (USDA)	1 head	60	4	13	Trace		91	2.3		1500	.29	.27	1.3	29
Lettuce, loose leaf or bunching varieties, leaves (USDA)	2 large	10	1	2	Trace		34	.7		950	.03	.04	.2	9
Mixed vegetables, canned (Del Monte)	1 cup	80	4	16	1		4%	8%	625	180%	4%	4%	4%	10%
Mixed vegetables, canned (Libby's)	1 cup	80	4	17	0		4%	6%		180%	6%	6%	4%	15%
Mixed vegetables, frozen (Birds Eye)	3.3 oz.	60	3	11	0		2%	2%	45	80%	6%	2%	4%	15%

FOOD	Measure or Weight	Food Energy Cal.	Proteins Gms.	Carbo-hydrates Gms.	Fat Gms.	Choles-terol Mg.	Calcium Mg.	Iron Mg.	Sodium Mg.	Vitamin A IU.	Thiamin Mg.	Ribo-flavin Mg.	Niacin C Mg.	Vitamin C Mg.
Mixed vegetables, frozen (Green Giant)	1 cup	90	4	16	1		4%	6%		80%	6%	2%	4%	15%
Mixed vegetables in butter sauce, frozen (Mexicorn)	1 cup	130	4	17	5		2%	6%		100%	6%	4%	4%	20%
Mushrooms, canned (USDA)	1 cup	40	5	6	Trace		15	1.2		Trace	.04	.6	4.8	4
Mushrooms, canned, whole, sliced, or pieces and stems (Green Giant)	2 oz.	14	1	2	0		★	★		★	★	2%	2%	★
Mushrooms in butter sauce, frozen (Green Giant)	2 oz.	30	1	2	2		★	★		2%	2%	2%	4%	2%
Mustard greens, cooked (USDA)	1 cup	35	3	6	1		193	2.5	25	8120	.11	.19	.9	68
Mustard greens, chopped frozen (Birds Eye)	3.3 oz.	18	2	3	0		2%	2%		110%	2%	4%	★	50%
Okra, cooked, 3 by 5/8 in. pod (USDA)	8 pods	25	2	5	Trace		78	.4		420	.11	.15	.8	17

VEGETABLES AND VEGETABLE PRODUCTS

FOOD	Measure or Weight	Food Energy Cal.	Proteins Gms.	Carbo- hydrates Gms.	Fat Gms.	Choles- terol Mg.	Calcium Mg.	Iron Mg.	Sodium Mg.	Vitamin A IU.	Thiamin Mg.	Ribo- flavin Mg.	Niacin C Mg.	Vitamin C Mg.
Okra, whole frozen (Birds Eye)	3.3 oz.	35	2	2	0		6%	★	2	10%	8%	10%	4%	30%
Onions, mature, raw, 2½ in. diameter (USDA)	1 onion	40	2	10	Trace		30	.6		40	.04	.04	.2	11
Onions, cooked (USDA)	1 cup	60	3	14	Trace		50	.8		80	.06	.06	.4	14
Onions, young green, small, without tops (USDA)	6 onions	20	1	5	Trace		20	.3		Trace	.02	.02	.2	12
Onions, small, whole, frozen (Birds Eye)	4 oz.	40	1	9	0		4%	★	10	★	2%	★	★	20%
Onions, creamed, small frozen (Green Giant)	1 cup	100	4	16	2		15%	2%		★	4%	8%	2%	15%
Onion rings, frozen (Mrs. Paul's)	2½ oz.	150	3	21	7		0	2%		0	4%	2%	8%	0
Parsley, raw, chopped (USDA)	1 tbsp.	Trace	Trace	Trace	Trace		8	.2		340	Trace	.01	Trace	7

FOOD	Measure or Weight	Food Energy Cal.	Proteins Gms.	Carbo-hydrates Gms.	Fat Gms.	Choles-terol Mg.	Calcium Mg.	Iron Mg.	Sodium Mg.	Vitamin A IU.	Thiamin Mg.	Ribo-flavin Mg.	Niacin C Mg.	Vitamin C Mg.
Parsnips, cooked (USDA)	1 cup	100	2	23	1		70	.9		50	.11	.12	.2	16
PEAS														
Peas, green, cooked (USDA)	1 cup	115	9	19	1		37	2.9		860	.44	.17	3.7	33
Peas, canned, solids and liquid (USDA)	1 cup	165	9	31	1		50	4.2		1120	.23	.13	2.2	22
Peas, green, immature, sweet (Libby's)	1 cup	120	7	23	1		2%	10%		20%	15%	10%	8%	30%
Early garden peas (Del Monte)	1 cup	110	7	20	1		4%	10%	670	20%	10%	8%	8%	35%
Early peas with onions (Green Giant)	1 cup	120	7	22	1		2%	10%		15%	6%	4%	4%	35%
Seasoned peas (Del Monte)	1 cup	120	27	25	1		4%	10%	605	20%	10%	8%	8%	35%
Small early peas (Le Sueur)	1 cup	110	6	19	1		2%	10%		15%	8%	4%	4%	35%
Small sweet peas (Le Sueur)	1 cup	100	6	17	1		2%	10%		15%	8%	4%	6%	30%

VEGETABLES AND VEGETABLE PRODUCTS

FOOD	Measure or Weight	Food Energy Cal.	Proteins Gms.	Carbohydrates Gms.	Fat Gms.	Cholesterol Mg.	Calcium Mg.	Iron Mg.	Sodium Mg.	Vitamin A IU.	Thiamin Mg.	Riboflavin Mg.	Niacin C Mg.	Vitamin C Mg.
Sweet peas (Green Giant)	1 cup	110	7	17	1		2%	10%		15%	8%	4%	6%	30%
Sweet peas (S & W Nutradiet)	½ cup	40	3	8	0		0	8%	9	6%	8%	2%	4%	18%
Sweet, tiny size peas (Del Monte)	1 cup	100	6	18	1		2%	15%	625	15%	15%	10%	6%	45%
Sweet peas with onions (Green Giant)	1 cup	110	7	17	1		2%	10%		15%	8%	4%	6%	30%
Sweetlets, small sweet peas (Green Giant)	1 cup	100	6	17	1		2%	10%		15%	8%	4%	6%	30%
Peas and carrots (Del Monte)	1 cup	100	5	19	0		4%	8%	630	420%	8%	8%	8%	25%
Peas and carrots (Libby's)	1 cup	100	6	20	1		4%	8%		200%	10%	8%	6%	15%
Peas and carrots (S & W Nutradiet)	½ cup	35	2	7	0		0	8%	9	90%	6%	2%	4%	12%
Sweet green peas, frozen (Birds Eye)	3.3 oz.	70	5	11	0		★	6%	110	15%	15%	4%	10%	35%

FOOD	Measure or Weight	Food Energy Cal.	Proteins Gms.	Carbohydrates Gms.	Fat Gms.	Cholesterol Mg.	Calcium Mg.	Iron Mg.	Sodium Mg.	Vitamin A IU.	Thiamin Mg.	Riboflavin Mg.	Niacin C Mg.	Vitamin C Mg.
Sweet peas, frozen (Green Giant)	1 cup	100	7	16	1		4%	10%		10%	10%	6%	10%	40%
Sweet peas in butter sauce, frozen (Le Sueur)	1 cup	150	7	18	6		4%	6%		25%	15%	4%	8%	45%
Sweet peas with onions in butter sauce, frozen (Le Sueur)	1 cup	140	6	16	6		4%	6%		20%	10%	6%	6%	25%
Sweet peas in cream sauce (Le Sueur)	1 cup	160	7	25	3		10%	6%		25%	10%	8%	6%	30%
Sweet peas with carrot points in cream sauce, frozen (Le Sueur)	1 cup	130	8	20	2		10%	10%		90%	15%	6%	6%	25%
PEPPERS														
Peppers, hot, red, without seeds, dried (ground chili powder, added seasonings) (USDA)	1 tbsp.	50	2	8	2		40	2.3		9750	.03	.17	1.3	2

VEGETABLES AND VEGETABLE PRODUCTS

FOOD	Measure or Weight	Food Energy Cal.	Proteins Gms.	Carbo-hydrates Gms.	Fat Gms.	Choles-terol Mg.	Calcium Mg.	Iron Mg.	Sodium Mg.	Vitamin A IU.	Thiamin Mg.	Ribo-flavin Mg.	Niacin C Mg.	Vitamin C Mg.
Peppers, sweet, raw, about 5 per pound, green pod without stem and seeds (USDA)	1 pod	15	1	4	Trace		7	.5		310	.06	.06	.4	94
Peppers, sweet, cooked, boiled, drained (USDA)	1 pod	15	1	3	Trace		7	.4		310	.05	.05	.4	70
POTATOES—Fresh and Canned														
Potatoes, medium, baked, peeled after baking (USDA)	1 potato	90	3	21	Trace		9	.7		Trace	.1	.04	1.7	20
Potatoes, medium, boiled, peeled after boiling (USDA)	1 potato	105	3	23	Trace		10	.8		Trace	.13	.05	2	22
Potatoes, medium, peeled before boiling (USDA)	1 potato	80	2	18	Trace		7	.6		Trace	.11	.04	1.4	20
Potatoes, new, canned (Del Monte)	1 cup	90	3	19	0		4%	6%	850	★	4%	2%	4%	50%

128

FOOD	Measure or Weight	Food Energy Cal.	Proteins Gms.	Carbohydrates Gms.	Fat Gms.	Cholesterol Mg.	Calcium Mg.	Iron Mg.	Sodium Mg.	Vitamin A IU.	Thiamin Mg.	Riboflavin Mg.	Niacin C Mg.	Vitamin C Mg.
French fried potatoes, 2 by ½ by ½ in., cooked in deep fat (USDA)	10 pieces	155	2	20	2		9	.7		Trace	.07	.04	1.8	12
— Frozen														
Baked potato with cheese (Holloway House)	6 oz.	300	5	36	15		6%	8%		*	2%	6%	6%	10%
Baked potato with sour cream (Holloway House)	6 oz.	280	5	36	13		4%	8%		*	*	4%	6%	10%
Bake-A-Tata with cheese (Holloway House)	5 oz.	220	4	27	11		4%	4%		*	*	2%	8%	4%
Bake-A-Tata with sour cream (Holloway House)	5 oz.	200	4	27	9		4%	2%		*	*	2%	8%	4%
French fried potatoes, frozen, heated (USDA)	10 pieces	125	2	19	1		5	1		Trace	.08	.01	1.5	12
Potatoes Au Gratin casserole (Green Giant)	1 cup	250	7	38	8		15%	4%		8%	2%	8%	4%	8%
Potatoes Romanoff casserole (Green Giant)	1 cup	250	4	35	11		10%	4%		8%	2%	8%	2%	10%

VEGETABLES AND VEGETABLE PRODUCTS

FOOD	Measure or Weight	Food Energy Cal.	Proteins Gms.	Carbohydrates Gms.	Fat Gms.	Cholesterol Mg.	Calcium Mg.	Iron Mg.	Sodium Mg.	Vitamin A IU.	Thiamin Mg.	Riboflavin Mg.	Niacin C Mg.	Vitamin C Mg.
Scalloped potatoes casserole (Green Giant)	1 cup	240	6	40	6		15%	2%		2%	2%	10%	4%	8%
— Mashed														
Mashed potatoes, milk added (USDA)	1 cup	125	4	25	1		47	.8		50	.16	.1	2	19
Mashed potatoes, milk and butter added (USDA)	1 cup	185	4	24	8		47	.8		330	.16	.1	1.9	18
Hungry Jack potatoes, mashed flakes (Pillsbury)	½ cup	170	3	18	10		4%	4%	440	8%	6%	4%	6%	40%
— Packaged, Dry														
Potatoes Au Gratin (Betty Crocker)	½ cup	90	2	19	1		4%	2%		★	★	2%	4%	6%
Potato Buds (Betty Crocker)	½ cup	60	2	14	0		★	★		★	★	★	6%	6%
Potatoes, creamed (Betty Crocker)	½ cup	80	1	17	1		★	★		★	★	★	4%	4%

FOOD	Measure or Weight	Food Energy Cal.	Proteins Gms.	Carbohydrates Gms.	Fat Gms.	Cholesterol Mg.	Calcium Mg.	Iron Mg.	Sodium Mg.	Vitamin A IU.	Thiamin Mg.	Riboflavin Mg.	Niacin C Mg.	Vitamin C Mg.
Potatoes, hash browns with onions (Betty Crocker)	½ cup	90	2	20	0		★	2%		★	★	★	10%	4%
Potatoes, julienne (Betty Crocker)	½ cup	80	2	16	1		2%	2%		★	★	2%	6%	4%
Potatoes, scalloped (Betty Crocker)	½ cup	90	2	19	1		2%	2%		★	★	★	4%	6%
Potatoes, sour cream 'n chive (Betty Crocker)	½ cup	90	2	17	1		2%	2%		★	★	2%	4%	4%
Potato chips, medium, 2 in. diameter (USDA)	10 chips	115	1	10	8		8	.4		Trace	.04	.01	1	3
Potato chips (Pringle's)	1 oz.	150	2	16	9		★	★		★	★	★	4%	25%
PUMPKINS TO SWEET POTATOES														
Pumpkin, canned (USDA)	1 cup	75	2	18	1		57	.9		14590	.07	.12	1.3	12
Pumpkin, canned (Del Monte)	1 cup	80	2	18	1		2%	8%	15	1200%	2%	6%	4%	15%
Pumpkin, canned (Libby's)	1 cup	80	2	20	1		6%	20%		600%	2%	8%	4%	15%

VEGETABLES AND VEGETABLE PRODUCTS

FOOD	Measure or Weight	Food Energy Cal.	Proteins Gms.	Carbohydrates Gms.	Fat Gms.	Cholesterol Mg.	Calcium Mg.	Iron Mg.	Sodium Mg.	Vitamin A IU.	Thiamin Mg.	Riboflavin Mg.	Niacin C Mg.	Vitamin C Mg.
Radishes, raw, small without tops (USDA)	4 radishes	5	Trace	1	Trace		12	.4		Trace	.01	.01	.1	10
Sauerkraut, canned, solids and liquid (USDA)	1 cup	45	2	9	Trace		85	1.2		120	.07	.09	.4	33
Sauerkraut, canned (Del Monte)	1 cup	50	2	11	0		6%	30%	1470	*	2%	2%	2%	60%
Sauerkraut, canned (Libby's)	1 cup	40	2	10	0		6%	15%		*	2%	2%	*	50%
Spinach, cooked (USDA)	1 cup	40	5	6	1		167	4		14580	.13	.25	1	50
Spinach, canned, drained solids (USDA)	1 cup	45	5	6	1		212	4.7		14400	.03	.21	.6	24
Spinach, canned (Del Monte)	1 cup	45	5	7	1		25%	15%	745	150%	2%	15%	2%	45%
Spinach, canned (Libby's)	1 cup	45	4	7	1		15%	15%		280%	2%	15%	2%	45%
Spinach in butter sauce, frozen (Le Sueur)	1 cup	90	5	6	5		15%	10%		100%	2%	8%	2%	60%

FOOD	Measure or Weight	Food Energy Cal.	Proteins Gms.	Carbo-hydrates Gms.	Fat Gms.	Choles-terol Mg.	Calcium Mg.	Iron Mg.	Sodium Mg.	Vitamin A IU.	Thiamin Mg.	Ribo-flavin Mg.	Niacin C Mg.	Vitamin C Mg.
Spinach, creamed, frozen (Birds Eye)	3 oz.	60	2	6	4		6%	4%	285	90%	4%	8%	★	15%
Spinach, creamed, frozen (Le Sueur)	1 cup	140	6	11	8		20%	10%		90%	4%	10%	2%	50%
Spinach, deviled, casserole, frozen (Green Giant)	1 cup	160	10	11	8		25%	15%		70%	6%	20%	4%	70%
Squash, cooked, summer, diced (USDA)	1 cup	30	2	7	Trace		52	.8		820	.1	.16	1.6	21
Squash, winter, baked (USDA)	1 cup	130	4	32	1		57	1.6		8610	.1	.27	1.4	27
Succotash, cream style, canned (Libby's)	1 cup	190	7	45	2		2%	8%		6%	4%	10%	6%	25%
Succotash, whole kernel, canned (Libby's)	1 cup	150	7	35	2		2%	8%		6%	4%	10%	6%	25%
Succotash, frozen (Birds Eye)	3.3 oz.	80	4	17	1		★	2%	25	4%	6%	2%	6%	20%
Sweet potatoes, medium, baked, peeled after baking (USDA)	1 potato	155	2	36	1		44	1		8910	.1	.07	.7	24

VEGETABLES AND VEGETABLE PRODUCTS

FOOD	Measure or Weight	Food Energy Cal.	Proteins Gms.	Carbo-hydrates Gms.	Fat Gms.	Choles-terol Mg.	Calcium Mg.	Iron Mg.	Sodium Mg.	Vitamin A IU.	Thiamin Mg.	Ribo-flavin Mg.	Niacin C Mg.	Vitamin C Mg.
Sweet potatoes, boiled, peeled after boiling (USDA)	1 potato	170	2	39	1		47	1		11610	.13	.09	.9	25
Sweet potatoes, candied (USDA)	1 potato	295	2	60	6		65	1.6		11030	.1	.08	.8	17
Sweet potatoes, canned (USDA)	1 cup	235	4	54	Trace		54	1.7		17000	.1	.1	1.4	30
TOMATOES														
Tomatoes, raw, approx. 3 in. diam. wt. 7 oz. (USDA)	1 tomato	40	2	9	Trace		24	.9		1640	.11	.07	1.3	42_7
Tomatoes, canned, solids and liquid (USDA)	1 cup	50	2	10	1		14	1.2		2170	.12	.07	1.7	41
Tomatoes, stewed, canned (Contadina)	1 cup	70	2	18	0		8%	6%		25%	8%	4%	8%	50%
Tomatoes, stewed, canned (Del Monte)	1 cup	70	2	16	0		6%	8%	675	20%	6%	4%	8%	60%

FOOD	Measure or Weight	Food Energy Cal.	Proteins Gms.	Carbo-hydrates Gms.	Fat Gms.	Choles-terol Mg.	Calcium Mg.	Iron Mg.	Sodium Mg.	Vitamin A IU.	Thiamin Mg.	Ribo-flavin Mg.	Niacin C Mg.	Vitamin C Mg.
Whole peeled tomatoes, canned (Del Monte)	1 cup	50	2	10	0		4%	4%	415	25%	8%	2%	6%	60%
Whole peeled tomatoes, canned (Hunt - Wesson)	4 oz.	20	1	5	0		2%	2%		10%	4%	2%	4%	25%
Whole peeled tomatoes, canned (Libby's)	1 cup	45	2	10	0		8%	4%		25%	8%	2%	6%	60%
Whole tomatoes, canned (S & W Nutradiet)	½ cup	25	1	5	0		4%	2%	15	15%	4%	2%	4%	30%
Tomato catsup (USDA)	1 cup	290	6	69	1		60	2.2		3820	.25	.19	4.4	41
Tomato catsup (USDA)	1 tbsp.	15	Trace	4	Trace		3	.1		210	.01	.01	.2	2
Tomato catsup (Del Monte)	¼ cup	60	1	16	0		*	2%	730	10%	2%	2%	4%	15%
Tomato ketchup (Hunt - Wesson)	1 tbsp.	18.2	.29	5.1	.03		2.2	.29		275	.015	.01	.24	5.7
Tomato juice, canned (USDA)	1 cup	45	2	10	Trace		17	2.2		1940	.12	.07	1.9	39
Tomato juice, canned (USDA)	1 glass, 6 oz.	35	2	8	Trace		13	1.6		1460	.09	.05	1.5	29

VEGETABLES AND VEGETABLE PRODUCTS

FOOD	Measure or Weight	Food Energy Cal.	Proteins Gms.	Carbo-hydrates Gms.	Fat Gms.	Choles-terol Mg.	Calcium Mg.	Iron Mg.	Sodium Mg.	Vitamin A IU.	Thiamin Mg.	Ribo-flavin Mg.	Niacin C Mg.	Vitamin C Mg.
Tomato juice, canned (Campbell)	6 oz.	35	1	7	0		2%	2%	325	15%	4%	2%	6%	40%
Tomato juice, canned (Contadina)	6 fl. oz.	35	1	8	0		*	4%		20%	4%	2%	6%	25%
Tomato juice, canned (Del Monte)	6 fl. oz.	35	1	8	0		*	6%	480	20%	4%	2%	6%	40%
Tomato juice, canned (Hunt - Wesson)	6 oz.	35	1.6	7.8	.18		12.8	1.6	646	1459	.09	.05	1.5	29
Tomato juice, canned (Libby's)	6 fl. oz.	35	1	8	0		*	4%		20%	4%	2%	6%	40%
Tomato juice, canned (S & W Nutradiet)	6 oz.	35	1	8	0		0	4%	10	15%	4%	2%	6%	35%
Tomato paste (Contadina)	6 oz.	150	6	35	0		4%	10%	25	90%	8%	10%	30%	80%
Tomato paste (Del Monte)	6 oz.	150	6	34	1		15%	15%	25	90%	20%	10%	25%	130%
Tomato paste (Hunt - Wesson)	3 oz.	70	3	14	0		2%	6%		40%	10%	35%	15%	50%

FOOD	Measure or Weight	Food Energy Cal.	Proteins Gms.	Carbohydrates Gms.	Fat Gms.	Cholesterol Mg.	Calcium Mg.	Iron Mg.	Sodium Mg.	Vitamin A IU.	Thiamin Mg.	Riboflavin Mg.	Niacin C Mg.	Vitamin C Mg.
Tomato puree (Contadina)	1 cup	90	4	20	0		2%	8%		50%	10%	6%	15%	50%
Tomato sauce (Contadina)	8 oz.	80	3	18	0		2%	10%		50%	8%	6%	15%	30%
Tomato sauce (Del Monte)	1 cup	180	3	217	1		4%	10%	1195	60%	10%	8%	10%	60%
Tomato sauce (Hunt - Wesson)	4 oz.	30	1	7	0		0	2%		20%	4%	8%	6%	15%
Tomato sauce with mushrooms (Del Monte)	1 cup	100	3	22	1		2%	10%	940	40%	10%	8%	10%	60%
Tomato sauce with mushrooms (Hunt - Wesson)	4 oz.	40	2	9	0		0	4%		25%	6%	10%	8%	25%
TURNIPS TO ZUCCHINI														
Turnips, cooked, diced (USDA)	1 cup	35	1	8	Trace		54	.6		Trace	.06	.08	.5	34
Turnip greens, cooked (USDA)	1 cup	30	3	5	Trace		252	1.5		8270	.15	.33	.7	68

VEGETABLES AND VEGETABLE PRODUCTS

FOOD	Measure or Weight	Food Energy Cal.	Proteins Gms.	Carbo-hydrates Gms.	Fat Gms.	Choles-terol Mg.	Calcium Mg.	Iron Mg.	Sodium Mg.	Vitamin A IU.	Thiamin Mg.	Ribo-flavin Mg.	Niacin C Mg.	Vitamin C Mg.
Turnip greens, chopped frozen (Birds Eye)	3.3 oz.	20	2	2	0		15%	6%	10	160%	2%	6%	2%	45%
Turnip greens, chopped with diced, turnips, frozen (Birds Eye)	3.3 oz.	20	2	3	0		10%	6%	15	130%	2%	4%	2%	45%
"V-8" cocktail vegetable juice (Campbell)	6 oz.	35	1	7	0		2%	2%	555	35%	4%	2%	6%	45%
"V-8" cocktail vegetable juice, low sodium (Campbell)	6 oz.	35	1	7	0		2%	2%	50	35%	4%	2%	6%	45%
Vegetable juice cocktail (S & W Nutradiet)	6 oz	35	1	0	8		0	4%	15	20%	4%	2%	6%	50%
Zucchini in tomato sauce, canned (Del Monte)	1 cup	60	2	16	0		4%	8%	850	30%	6%	6%	4%	15%
Zucchini parmesan, frozen (Mrs. Paul's)	6 oz.	320	4	62	7		4%	4%		6%	8%	4%	8%	4%

FRUITS AND FRUIT PRODUCTS

FRUITS AND FRUIT PRODUCTS

FOOD	Measure or Weight	Food Energy Cal.	Proteins Gms.	Carbo-hydrates Gms.	Fat Gms.	Choles-terol Mg.	Calcium Mg.	Iron Mg.	Sodium Mg.	Vitamin A IU.	Thiamin Mg.	Ribo-flavin Mg.	Niacin C Mg.	Vitamin C Mg.
Apples, raw, about 3 per lb.₅ (USDA)	1 apple	70	Trace	18	Trace		8	.4		50	.04	.02	.1	3
Apples, evaporated, uncooked (Del Monte)	2 oz.	140	0	37	0		★	4%	60	★	★	4%	2%	★
Apple cider and cranberry juice, sweetened (Ocean Spray)	6 fl. oz.	110	0	28	0		★	2%		★	★	2%	★	★
Apple fritters, frozen (Mrs. Paul's)	2	240	3	32	12		0	4%		0	2%	12%	0	8%
Apple juice, bottled or canned (USDA)	1 cup	120	Trace	30	Trace		15	1.5		—	.02	.05	.2	2
Apple juice (White House)	6 fl. oz.	87	0	22	0		★	★		★	★	★	★	★
Apple fruit drink (Hi - C)	6 oz.	90		22			Trace	.39	11.7	—	Trace	Trace	Trace	60
Applesauce, canned, sweetened (USDA)	1 cup	230	1	61	Trace		10	1.3		100	.05	.03	.1	3₈

FOOD	Measure or Weight	Food Energy Cal.	Proteins Gms.	Carbohydrates Gms.	Fat Gms.	Cholesterol Mg.	Calcium Mg.	Iron Mg.	Sodium Mg.	Vitamin A IU.	Thiamin Mg.	Riboflavin Mg.	Niacin C Mg.	Vitamin C Mg.
Applesauce, canned, unsweetened or artifically sweetened (USDA)	1 cup	100	1	26	Trace		10	1.2		100	.05	.02	.1	2₈
Applesauce (Del Monte)	1 cup	170	0	47	0		★	4%		★	2%	4%	2%	6%
Apple sauce (S & W Nutradiet)	½ cup	55	0	14	0		0	0		0	0	0	0	0
Apple sauce, regular or chunky (White House)	4 oz.	103	0	27	0		★	★		★	★	★	★	★
Apple sauce, dietetic (White House)	4 oz.	50	0	12	0		★	★		★	★	★	★	★
Apples, sliced, packed with water and sugar (White House)	4 oz.	54	0	14	0		★	★		★	★	★	★	★
Apple rings, spiced (White House)	1 ring	19	0	5	0		★	★		★	★	★	★	★
Apricots, raw, about 12 per lb. (USDA)	3 apricots	55	1	14	Trace		18	.5		2890	.03	.04	.7	10
Apricots, canned in heavy syrup (USDA)	1 cup	220	2	57	Trace		28	.8		4510	.05	.06	.9	10

FRUITS AND FRUIT PRODUCTS

FOOD	Measure or Weight	Food Energy Cal.	Proteins Gms.	Carbo-hydrates Gms.	Fat Gms.	Choles-terol Mg.	Calcium Mg.	Iron Mg.	Sodium Mg.	Vitamin A IU.	Thiamin Mg.	Ribo-flavin Mg.	Niacin C Mg.	Vitamin C Mg.
Apricots, halves, unpeeled (Del Monte)	1 cup	200	1	52	0		2%	4%	15	45%	4%	2%	6%	10%
Apricots, halves (S & W Nutradiet)	½ cup	35	0	9	0		0%	2%		34%	2%	2%	2%	4%
Apricots, whole, peeled, (Del Monte)	1 cup	200	1	53	0		2%	4%	40	35%	2%	4%	4%	10%
Apricots, solids & liquids, heavy syrup (Libby's)	1 cup	200	1	54	0		2%	2%		60%	4%	2%	2%	10%
Apricots, dried, uncooked, 40 halves per cup (USDA)	1 cup	390	8	100	1		100	8.2		16350	.02	.23	4.9	19
Apricots, dried, uncooked (Del Monte)	2 oz.	140	2	35	0		2%	15%		90%	★	4%	8%	★
Apricots, unsweetened, fruit and liquid, cooked (USDA)	1 cup	240	5	62	1		63	5.1		8550	.01	.13	2.8	8

FOOD	Measure or Weight	Food Energy Cal.	Proteins Gms.	Carbo-hydrates Gms.	Fat Gms.	Choles-terol Mg.	Calcium Mg.	Iron Mg.	Sodium Mg.	Vitamin A IU.	Thiamin Mg.	Ribo-flavin Mg.	Niacin C Mg.	Vitamin C Mg.
Apricot nectar, canned (USDA)	1 cup	140	1	37	Trace		23	.5		2380	.03	.03	.5	8[8]
Apricot nectar (Del Monte)	6 fl. oz.	100	1	26	0		*	4%		40%	2%	2%	2%	50%
Apricot nectar (S & W Nutradiet)	6 oz.	33	1	9	0		0	2%		60%	0	2%	2%	2%
Apricot and pineapple nectar (S & W Nutradiet)	6 oz.	49	0	12	0		0	4%		40%	2%	0	2%	2%
Avocados, whole fruit, raw, California, mid and late winter, 3⅛ in. diam. (USDA)	1 avocado	370	5	13	37		22	1.3		630	.24	.43	3.5	30
Avocados, whole fruit, raw, Florida, late summer, fall, 3⅝ in. diam. (USDA)	1 avocado	390	4	27	33		30	1.8		880	.33	.61	4.9	43
Bananas, raw, medium size [5] (USDA)	1 banana	100	1	26	Trace		10	.8		230	.06	.07	.8	12

FRUITS AND FRUIT PRODUCTS

FOOD	Measure or Weight	Food Energy Cal.	Proteins Gms.	Carbo-hydrates Gms.	Fat Gms.	Choles-terol Mg.	Calcium Mg.	Iron Mg.	Sodium Mg.	Vitamin A IU.	Thiamin Mg.	Ribo-flavin Mg.	Niacin C Mg.	Vitamin C Mg.
Banana flakes (USDA)	1 cup	340	4	89	1		32	2.8		760	.18	.24	2.8	7
Blackberries, raw (USDA)	1 cup	85	2	19	1		46	1.3		290	.05	.06	.5	30
Blueberries, raw (USDA)	1 cup	85	1	21	1		21	1.4		140	.04	.08	.6	20
Cantaloupes, raw, medium 5-in. diam. about 1⅔ lbs.5	½ melon	60	1	14	Trace		27	.8		6540g	.08	.06	1.2	63
Cherries, canned, red, sour, pitted, water pack (USDA)	1 cup	105	2	26	Trace		37	.7		1660	.07	.05	.5	12
Cherries, light sweet with pits, Royal Anne (Del Monte)	1 cup	190	1	51	0		★	2%		4%	2%	4%	4%	10%
Cherries, water pack, Royal Anne (S & W Nutradiet)	½ cup	70	0	17	0		0	2%		4%	0	0	0	0
Cherries, dark, sweet with pits (Del Monte)	1 cup	180	1	48	1		2%	4%		8%	4%	4%	4%	15%

FOOD	Measure or Weight	Food Energy Cal.	Proteins Gms.	Carbo-hydrates Gms.	Fat Gms.	Choles-terol Mg.	Calcium Mg.	Iron Mg.	Sodium Mg.	Vitamin A IU.	Thiamin Mg.	Ribo-flavin Mg.	Niacin C Mg.	Vitamin C Mg.
Cherries, dark, sweet (S & W Nutradiet)	½ cup	70	0	17	0		0	4%		2%	0	0	0	0
Cherries, pitted, dark, sweet (Del Monte)	1 cup	190	1	50	1		2%	4%		8%	4%	4%	4%	15%
Cherry fruit drink (Hi - C)	6 fl. oz.	90					Trace	Trace	4.1	Trace	Trace	Trace	Trace	60
Cranapple, cranberry apple drink (Ocean Spray)	6 fl. oz.	140	0	34	0		★	★		★	★	★	★	100%
Cranapple, low calorie (Ocean Spray)	6 fl. oz.	30	0	7	0		★	★		★	★	★	★	100%
Cranberries, fresh fruit, - about ½ cup (Ocean Spray)	2 oz.	25	0	6	0		★	★		★	★	★	★	10%
Cranberry juice cocktail, canned (USDA)	1 cup	165	Trace	42	Trace		13	.8		Trace	.03	.03	.1	40₁₀
Cranberry juice cocktail, (Ocean Spray)	6 fl. oz.	110	0	28	0		★	★		★	★	★	★	100%

FRUITS AND FRUIT PRODUCTS

FOOD	Measure or Weight	Food Energy Cal.	Proteins Gms.	Carbo-hydrates Gms.	Fat Gms.	Choles-terol Mg.	Calcium Mg.	Iron Mg.	Sodium Mg.	Vitamin A IU.	Thiamin Mg.	Ribo-flavin Mg.	Niacin C Mg.	Vitamin C Mg.
Cranberry juice cocktail, low calorie (Ocean Spray)	6 fl. oz.	35	0	9	0		★	★		★	★	★	★	100%
Cranberry sauce, sweetened, canned, strained (USDA)	1 cup	405	Trace	104	1		17	.6		60	.03	.03	.1	6
Cranberry orange relish (Ocean Spray)	2 oz.	100	0	26	0		★	★		★	★	★	★	★
Cranberry sauce, jellied (Ocean Spray)	2 oz.	90	0	22	0		★	★		★	★	★	★	★
Cranberry sauce, whole (Ocean Spray)	2 oz.	90	0	21	0		★	★		★	★	★	★	★
Crangrape, grape cranberry drink (Ocean Spray)	6 fl. oz.	120	0	31	0		★	★		★	★	★	★	100%
Cranicot, cranberry apricot juice drink (Ocean Spray)	6 fl. oz.	130	0	33	0		★	★		★	★	★	★	★

FOOD	Measure or Weight	Food Energy Cal.	Proteins Gms.	Carbo-hydrates Gms.	Fat Gms.	Choles-terol Mg.	Calcium Mg.	Iron Mg.	Sodium Mg.	Vitamin A IU.	Thiamin Mg.	Ribo-flavin Mg.	Niacin C Mg.	Vitamin C Mg.
Cranprune, cranberry prune juice drink (Ocean Spray)	6 fl. oz.	130	0	33	0		★	★		★	★	★	★	100%
Currants, zante (Del Monte)	½ cup	190	3	48	0		4%	15%		★	8%	6%	6%	4%
Dates, pitted, cut (USDA)	1 cup	490	4	130	1		105	5.3		90	.16	.17	3.9	0
Figs, dried, large, 2 by 1 in. (USDA)	1 fig	60	1	15	Trace		26	.6		20	.02	.02	.1	0
Figs, whole (Del Monte)	1 cup	210	1	55	0		6%	2%		★	2%	4%	4%	4%
Fruit cocktail, canned, in heavy syrup (USDA)	1 cup	195	1	50	Trace		23	1		360	.05	.03	1.3	5
Fruit cocktail (Del Monte)	1 cup	170	1	45	0		★	4%		8%	2%	4%	6%	8%
Fruit cocktail (Hunt Wesson)	1 cup	178	1	46.8	.25		22.9	1	12.7	356	.05	.025	1	5.1
Fruit cocktail (Libby's)	1 cup	170	1	45	0		★	2%		8%	2%	2%	2%	8%
Fruit cocktail (S & W Nutradiet)	½ cup	40	0	10	0		0	0		4%	0	0	2%	4%

FRUITS AND FRUIT PRODUCTS

FOOD	Measure or Weight	Food Energy Cal.	Proteins Gms.	Carbo-hydrates Gms.	Fat Gms.	Choles-terol Mg.	Calcium Mg.	Iron Mg.	Sodium Mg.	Vitamin A IU.	Thiamin Mg.	Ribo-flavin Mg.	Niacin C Mg.	Vitamin C Mg.
Fruits for salad (Del Monte)	1 cup	170	1	46	0		★	4%		10%	2%	4%	6%	10%
Fruits for salad (Libby's)	1 cup	180	1	48	0		★	2%		15%	2%	2%	2%	10%
Fruit salad, tropical (Del Monte)	1 cup	200	1	52	0		2%	6%		6%	8%	6%	6%	60%
Fruit, salad (S & W Nutradiet)	½ cup	50	0	11	0		0	0		15%	0	0	2%	4%
Grapefruit, raw, medium, 3¾ in. diam.5 (USDA)	½ grapefruit	45	1	12	Trace		19	.5		10	.05	.02	.2	44
Grapefruit, raw, medium, pink or red (USDA)	½ grapefruit	50	1	13	Trace		20	.5		540	.05	.02	.2	44
Grapefruit, canned, syrup pack (USDA)	1 cup	180	2	45	Trace		33	.8		30	.08	.05	.5	76
Grapefruit, sections in juice (Del Monte)	1 cup	90	1	21	0		2%	4%		★	6%	★	2%	100%

148

FOOD	Measure or Weight	Food Energy Cal.	Proteins Gms.	Carbo-hydrates Gms.	Fat Gms.	Choles-terol Mg.	Calcium Mg.	Iron Mg.	Sodium Mg.	Vitamin A IU.	Thiamin Mg.	Ribo-flavin Mg.	Niacin Mg.	Vitamin C Mg.
Grapefruit, sections in syrup (Del Monte)	1 cup	140	1	35	0		2%	4%		★	4%	2%	2%	80%
Grapefruit, juice pack, S & W Nutradiet	½ cup	40	0	9	0		0	0		0	0	0	0	60%
Grapefruit juice, fresh (USDA)	1 cup	95	1	23	Trace		22	.5		11	.09	.04	.4	92
Grapefruit juice, sweetened, white, canned (USDA)	1 cup	130	1	32	Trace		20	1		20	.07	.04	.4	78
Grapefruit juice, sweetened, (Del Monte)	6 fl. oz.	80	1	21	0		★	2%		★	4%	2%	2%	80%
Grapefruit juice, white, unsweetened, canned (USDA)	1 cup	100	1	24	Trace		20	1		20	.07	.04	.4	84
Grapefruit juice, unsweetened (Del Monte)	6 fl. oz.	70	1	17	0		★	2%		★	4%	2%	2%	90%
Grapefruit juice, frozen concentrate, unsweetened diluted with 3 parts water by volume (USDA)	1 cup	100	1	24	Trace		25	.2		20	.1	.04	.5	96

FRUITS AND FRUIT PRODUCTS

FOOD	Measure or Weight	Food Energy Cal.	Proteins Gms.	Carbo-hydrates Gms.	Fat Gms.	Choles-terol Mg.	Calcium Mg.	Iron Mg.	Sodium Mg.	Vitamin A IU.	Thiamin Mg.	Ribo-flavin Mg.	Niacin C Mg.	Vitamin C Mg.
Grapefruit juice, frozen (Minute Maid)	6 oz.	75		18.3			18	.2		16	.07	.031	.36	72
Grapefruit juice, dehydrated crystals prepared with water (USDA)	1 cup	100	1	24	Trace		22	.2		20	.1	.05	.5	91
Grapes, raw₅, American type, slip skin (USDA)	1 cup	65	1	15	1		15	.4		100	.05	.03	.2	3
Grapes, raw₅, European type, adherant skin (USDA)	1 cup	95	1	25	Trace		17	.6		140	.07	.04	.4	6
Grape juice, canned or bottled (USDA)	1 cup	165	1	42	Trace		28	.8		—	.1	.05	.5	Trace
Grape juice drink, canned (USDA)	1 cup	135	Trace	35	Trace		8	.3		—	.03	.03	3	12
Grape flavor instant breakfast drink (Tang)	4 fl. oz.	50	0	14	0		2%	★	5	20%	★	★	★	100%
Grape fruit drink (Hi - C)	6 oz.	98	0	23	Trace		Trace	Trace	.41	Trace	Trace	Trace	Trace	60

150

FOOD	Measure or Weight	Food Energy Cal.	Proteins Gms.	Carbohydrates Gms.	Fat Gms.	Cholesterol Mg.	Calcium Mg.	Iron Mg.	Sodium Mg.	Vitamin A IU.	Thiamin Mg.	Riboflavin Mg.	Niacin C Mg.	Vitamin C Mg.
Grape juice, frozen, concentrate, sweetened, diluted with 3 parts water by volume (USDA)	1 cup	135	1	33	Trace		8	.3		10		.08	5	12
Grape juice, frozen, sweetened (Minute Maid)	6 oz.	99		25			5.4	.22	1.61	11	.03	.054	.37	8
Lemons, raw, 2 1/8 in. diam., size 165$_5$ used for juice (USDA)	1 lemon	20	1	6	Trace		19	.4		10	.03	.01	.1	39
Lemon juice, raw (USDA)	1 cup	60	1	20	Trace		17	.5		50	.07	.02	.2	112
Lemonade concentrate, frozen, diluted with 4 1/3 parts water, by volume (USDA)	1 cup	110	Trace	28	Trace		2	Trace		Trace	Trace	.02	.2	17
Lemonade, frozen (Minute Maid)	6 oz.	74		19.6	.01		1.5	.07	.75	8	.007	.011	.11	11
Lime juice, fresh (USDA)	1 cup	65	1	22	Trace		22	.5		20	.05	.02	.2	79
Lime juice, canned, unsweetened (USDA)	1 cup	65	1	22	Trace		22	.5		20	.05	.02	.2	52

FRUITS AND FRUIT PRODUCTS

FOOD	Measure or Weight	Food Energy Cal.	Proteins Gms.	Carbo-hydrates Gms.	Fat Gms.	Choles-terol Mg.	Calcium Mg.	Iron Mg.	Sodium Mg.	Vitamin A IU.	Thiamin Mg.	Ribo-flavin Mg.	Niacin C Mg.	Vitamin C Mg.
Limeade concentrate, frozen, diluted with 4⅓ parts water by volume (USDA)	1 cup	100	Trace	27	Trace		2	Trace		Trace	Trace	Trace	Trace	5
Limeade, frozen (Minute Maid)	6 oz.	75		20.1	.01		2	.04	Trace	Trace	.004	.004	.04	5
Mixed fruit, frozen (Birds Eye)	5 oz.	130	1	34	0		★	2%	5	10%	★	2%	2%	45%
Oranges, raw, 2⅝ in. diam., all commercial varieties (USDA)	1 orange	65	1	16	Trace		54	.5		260	.13	.05	.5	66
Orange fruit drink (Hi - C)	6 oz.	98		24	Trace		Trace	Trace	57.5	Trace	Trace	Trace	Trace	60
Orange juice, fresh, all varieties (USDA)	1 cup	110	2	26	1		27	.5		500	.22	.07	1	124
Orange juice, canned, unsweetened (USDA)	1 cup	120	2	28	Trace		25	1		500	.17	.05	.7	100
Orange juice, sweetened (Del Monte)	6 fl. oz.	70	1	18	0		★	4%		6	6%	2%	2%	80%

FOOD	Measure or Weight	Food Energy Cal.	Proteins Gms.	Carbo-hydrates Gms.	Fat Gms.	Choles-terol Mg.	Calcium Mg.	Iron Mg.	Sodium Mg.	Vitamin A IU.	Thiamin Mg.	Ribo-flavin Mg.	Niacin C Mg.	Vitamin C Mg.
Orange juice, unsweetened (Del Monte)	6 fl. oz.	80	1	19	0		★	4%		4%	6%	2%	2%	120%
Orange juice, frozen concentrate diluted with 3 parts water by volume (USDA)	1 cup	120	2	29	Trace		25	.2		550	.22	.02	1	120
Orange juice, frozen (Minute Maid)	6 oz.	90	1	21.4	.06		19	.22	1.14	406	.17	.029	.68	90
Orange juice, frozen (Snow Crop)	6 oz.	90	1	21.4	.06		19	.22	1.14	406	.17	.029	.68	90
Orange juice, Awake, imitation, frozen (Birds Eye)	6 fl. oz.	90	0	23	0		4%	★	10	4%	10%	★	★	150%
Orange Plus, breakfast beverage, frozen (Birds Eye)	6 fl. oz.	100	1	25	0		2%	★	15	4%	10%	2%	2%	150%
Orange juice, dehydrated crystals, prepared with water (USDA)	1 cup	115	2	27	1		25	.5		500	.2	.07	1	109
Orange instant breakfast drink (Start)	4 fl. oz.	50	0	13	0		6%	★	7	20%	★	★	★	100%

FRUITS AND FRUIT PRODUCTS

FOOD	Measure or Weight	Food Energy Cal.	Proteins Gms.	Carbo-hydrates Gms.	Fat Gms.	Choles-terol Mg.	Calcium Mg.	Iron Mg.	Sodium Mg.	Vitamin A IU.	Thiamin Mg.	Ribo-flavin Mg.	Niacin C Mg.	Vitamin C Mg.
Orange instant breakfast drink (Tang)	4 fl. oz.	50	0	13	0		6%	★	7	20%	★	★	★	100%
Orange-apricot drink (USDA)	1 cup	125	1	32	Trace		12	.2		1440	.05	.02	.5	40₁₀
Orange and grapefruit juice, canned, sweetened (Del Monte)	6 fl. oz.	80	1	20	0		★	4%		★	4%	2%	4%	60%
Orange and grapefruit juice, canned, unsweetened (Del Monte)	6 fl. oz.	80	1	19	0		★	4%		4%	6%	2%	2%	80%
Orange and grapefruit juice, frozen concentrate diluted with 3 parts water by volume (USDA)	1 cup	110	1	26	Trace		20	.2	.56	270	.16	.02	.8	102
Orange pineapple fruit drink (Hi - C)	6 oz.	98	1	25	Trace		Trace	Trace		576	Trace	Trace	Trace	60
Papayas, ½ inch cubes (USDA)	1 cup	70	1	18	Trace		36	.5		3190	.07	.08	.5	102

FOOD	Measure or Weight	Food Energy Cal.	Proteins Gms.	Carbo-hydrates Gms.	Fat Gms.	Choles-terol Mg.	Calcium Mg.	Iron Mg.	Sodium Mg.	Vitamin A IU.	Thiamin Mg.	Ribo-flavin Mg.	Niacin C Mg.	Vitamin C Mg.
Peaches, raw, whole, medium, 2 in. diam., about 4 per lb. (USDA)	1 peach	35	1	10	Trace		9	.5		1320_{13}	.02	.05	1	7
Peaches, raw, sliced (USDA)	1 cup	65	1	16	Trace		15	.8		2230_{13}	.03	.08	1.6	12
Peaches, canned, yellow-fleshed, solids and liquids, syrup pack, halves or slices (USDA)	1 cup	200	1	52	Trace		10	.8		1100	.02	.06	1.4	7
Peaches (Hunt Wesson)	1 cup	192	1	50.4	.26		10	.8	5.1	1100	.026	.05	1.5	7.7
Peaches, cling, solids and liquid, heavy syrup (Libby's)	1 cup	170	1	45	0		★	2%		20%	★	2%	6%	15%
Peaches, cling halves (S & W Nutradiet)	½ cup	30	0	8	0		0	0		10%	0	0	4%	6%
Peaches, freestone halves or slices (Del Monte)	1 cup	170	1	45	0		★	2%	20	4%	2%	4%	10%	4%
Peaches, spiced, with pits (Del Monte)	7¼ oz.	150	1	40	0		★	2%		10%	★	4%	4%	2%

FRUITS AND FRUIT PRODUCTS

FOOD	Measure or Weight	Food Energy Cal.	Proteins Gms.	Carbo-hydrates Gms.	Fat Gms.	Choles-terol Mg.	Calcium Mg.	Iron Mg.	Sodium Mg.	Vitamin A IU.	Thiamin Mg.	Ribo-flavin Mg.	Niacin C Mg.	Vitamin C Mg.
Peaches, yellow cling halves or slices (Del Monte)	1 cup	170	1	45	0		★	2%		20%	★	4%	8%	15%
Peaches, canned, water pack (USDA)	1 cup	75	1	20	Trace		10	.7		1100	.02	.06	1.4	7
Peaches, dried, uncooked (USDA)	1 cup	420	5	109	1		77	9.6		6240	.02	.31	8.5	28
Peaches, dried, uncooked (Del Monte)	2 oz.	140	2	35	0		★	10%		25	★	6%	10%	★
Peaches, dried, cooked, unsweetened, 10-12 halves and juice (USDA)	1 cup	220	3	58	1		41	5.1		3290	.01	.15	4.2	6
Peaches, frozen, carton 12 oz. not thawed (USDA)	1 carton	300	1	77	Trace		14	1.7		.210	.03	.14	2.4	135₁₄
Peaches, frozen (Birds Eye)	5 oz.	130	1	34	0		★	2%		8%	★	2%	4%	45%
Peach nectar (Del Monte)	6 fl. oz.	100	1	27	0		★	2%		8%	★	2%	4%	50%

156

FOOD	Measure or Weight	Food Energy Cal.	Proteins Gms.	Carbohydrates Gms.	Fat Gms.	Cholesterol Mg.	Calcium Mg.	Iron Mg.	Sodium Mg.	Vitamin A IU.	Thiamin Mg.	Riboflavin Mg.	Niacin C Mg.	Vitamin C Mg.
Peach nectar (S & W Nutradiet)	6 oz.	40	1	9	0		0	4%		8%	0	0	2%	0
Pears, raw, 3 by 2½ in. diam.5 (USDA)	1 pear	100	1	25	1		13	.5		30	.04	.07	.2	7
Pears, canned, solids and liquid, syrup pack, heavy, halves or slices (USDA)	1 cup	195	1	50	1		13	.5		Trace	.03	.05	.3	4
Pears, canned, Bartlett halves or slices (Del Monte)	1 cup	160	0	43	0		★	2%	15	★	★	2%	2%	4%
Pears, canned (Hunt Wesson)	1 cup	181	.5	46.3	.5		12.7	.5	2.5	—	.025	.05	.25	2.5
Pears, canned solids and liquid, heavy syrup (Libby's)	1 cup	170	0	44	0		★	2%		★	★	★	★	4%
Pear halves, water pack (S & W Nutradiet)	½ cup	40	0	10	0		0	2%		0	0	2%	0	2%
Pears, dried, uncooked (Del Monte)	2 oz.	150	1	40	0		★	6%		★	★	4%	2%	★

FRUITS AND FRUIT PRODUCTS

FOOD	Measure or Weight	Food Energy Cal.	Proteins Gms.	Carbo-hydrates Gms.	Fat Gms.	Choles-terol Mg.	Calcium Mg.	Iron Mg.	Sodium Mg.	Vitamin A IU.	Thiamin Mg.	Ribo-flavin Mg.	Niacin C Mg.	Vitamin C Mg.
Pear nectar (Del Monte)	6 fl. oz.	110	0	30	0		★	20%		★	★	★	2%	50%
Pear nectar (S & W Nutradiet)	6 oz.	27	0	6	0		0	4%		0	0	0	0	0
Pineapple, raw, diced (USDA)	1 cup	75	1	19	Trace		24	.7		100	.12	.04	.3	24
Pineapple, canned, heavy syrup pack, solids and liquid, crushed (USDA)	1 cup	195	1	50	Trace		29	.8		120	.2	.06	.5	17
Pineapple, crushed, chunks or medium slices in juice (Del Monte)	1 cup	140	1	35	0		2%	4%		2%	10%	2%	2%	10%
Pineapple, tidbits, juice pack (S & W Nutradiet)	½ cup	70	0	17	0		0	2%		0	4%	0	0	4%
Pineapple, sliced, slices and juice (USDA)	2 small or 1 large	90	Trace	24	Trace		13	.4		50	.09	.03	.2	8
Pineapple, crushed, chunks or medium slices in syrup (Del Monte)	1 cup	190	1	49	0		2%	6%		2%	10%	2%	2%	10%

158

FOOD	Measure or Weight	Food Energy Cal.	Proteins Gms.	Carbohydrates Gms.	Fat Gms.	Cholesterol Mg.	Calcium Mg.	Iron Mg.	Sodium Mg.	Vitamin A IU.	Thiamin Mg.	Riboflavin Mg.	Niacin C Mg.	Vitamin C Mg.
Pineapple, sliced, juice pack (S & W Nutradiet)	1 slice	70	0	17	0		0	2%		0	4%	0	0	4%
Pineapple juice, canned (USDA)	1 cup	135	1	34	Trace		37	.7		120	.12	.04	.5	22[8]
Pineapple juice, vitamin C fortified (Del Monte)	6 fl. oz.	100	0	25	0		2%	2%		★	6%	2%	2%	100%
Pineapple grapefruit juice drink (Del Monte)	6 fl. oz.	90	0	24	0		★	2%	45	★	2%	2%	★	50%
Pineapple orange juice drink (Del Monte)	6 fl. oz.	90	0	23	0		★	2%		15%	2%	2%	★	50%
Pineapple pink grapefruit juice drink (Del Monte)	6 fl. oz.	90	0	24	0		★	2%	45	★	2%	2%	★	50%
Plums, all except prunes, raw, 2-in. diam., about 2 ounces[5] (USDA)	1 plum	25	Trace	7	Trace		7	.3		140	.02	.02	.3	3
Plums, canned, syrup pack (Italian prunes) with pits and juice[5] (USDA)	1 cup	205	1	53	Trace		22	2.2		2970	.05	.05	.9	4

FRUITS AND FRUIT PRODUCTS

FOOD	Measure or Weight	Food Energy Cal.	Proteins Gms.	Carbo-hydrates Gms.	Fat Gms.	Choles-terol Mg.	Calcium Mg.	Iron Mg.	Sodium Mg.	Vitamin A IU.	Thiamin Mg.	Ribo-flavin Mg.	Niacin C Mg.	Vitamin C Mg.
Plums, purple with pits (Del Monte)	1 cup	190	1	52	0		2%	2%		30%	4%	6%	6%	2%
Purple plums, water pack (S & W Nutradiet)	½ cup	55	0	17	0		0	0		25%	0	2%	0	4%
Prunes, dried, "softenized" medium, uncooked5 (USDA)	4 prunes	70	1	18	Trace		14	1.1		440	.02	.04	.4	1
Prunes, dried, uncooked with pits (Del Monte)	2 oz.	120	1	31	1		2%	6%		20%	2%	6%	4%	★
Prunes, dried, pitted (Del Monte)	2 oz.	140	1	36	0		2%	6%		10%	2%	6%	4%	★
Prunes, cooked, unsweetened, 17-18 prunes and ⅓ cup liquid5 (USDA)	1 cup	295	2	78	1		60	4.5		1860	.08	.18	1.7	2
Prunes, stewed with pits (Del Monte)	1 cup	230	2	60	1		2%	4%		40%	4%	15%	8%	10%

FOOD	Measure or Weight	Food Energy Cal.	Proteins Gms.	Carbohydrates Gms.	Fat Gms.	Cholesterol Mg.	Calcium Mg.	Iron Mg.	Sodium Mg.	Vitamin A IU.	Thiamin Mg.	Riboflavin Mg.	Niacin C Mg.	Vitamin C Mg.
Prune juice, canned or bottled (USDA)	1 cup	200	1	49	Trace		36	10.5		—	.03	.03	1	5
Prune juice, unsweetened (Bennett's)	8 oz.	195	1	50	0				5					
Prune juice (Del Monte)	6 fl. oz.	120	1	33	0		★	8%		★	2%	15%	6%	10%
Raisins, seedless, ½ oz. or 1½ tbsp. per pkg. (USDA)	1 pkg.	40	Trace	11	Trace		9	.5		Trace	.02	.01	.1	Trace
Raisins, cup, pressed down (USDA)	1 cup	480	4	128	Trace		102	5.8		30	.18	.13	.8	2
Raisins, golden seedless (Del Monte)	3 oz.	260	3	68	0		4%	8%		★	★	10%	4%	★
Raisins, muscat (Del Monte)	3 oz.	250	2	66	0		2%	2%	25	★	6%	6%	4%	★
Raspberries, red, raw (USDA)	1 cup	70	1	17	1		27	1.1		160	.04	.11	1.1	31
Raspberries, frozen, 10 oz. carton, not thawed (USDA)	1 carton	275	2	70	1		37	1.7		200	.06	.17	1.7	59

FRUITS AND FRUIT PRODUCTS

FOOD	Measure or Weight	Food Energy Cal.	Proteins Gms.	Carbohydrates Gms.	Fat Gms.	Cholesterol Mg.	Calcium Mg.	Iron Mg.	Sodium Mg.	Vitamin A IU.	Thiamin Mg.	Riboflavin Mg.	Niacin C Mg.	Vitamin C Mg.
Red Raspberries, frozen (Birds Eye)	5 oz.	140	1	35	0		★	6%	1	★	★	4%	2%	35%
Rhubarb, cooked, sugar added (USDA)	1 cup	385	1	98	Trace		212	1.6		220	.06	.15	.7	17
Strawberries, raw, capped (USDA)	1 cup	55	1	13	1		31	1.5		90	.04	.1	1	88
Strawberries, canned, water pack (S & W Nutradiet)	½ cup	35	0	7	0		2%	2%		0	0	0	0	50%
Strawberries, frozen, 10 oz. carton, not thawed (USDA)	1 carton	310	1	79	1		40	2		90	.06	.17	1.5	150
Strawberries, sliced, frozen (Birds Eye)	5 oz.	180	1	48	0		★	2%	4	★	★	6%	2%	80%
Strawberries, whole, frozen (Birds Eye)	4 oz.	80	1	23	0		★	2%	1	★	★	2%	★	70%
Strawberry halves, frozen (Birds Eye)	5.3 oz.	170	1	48	0		★	4%	3	★	★	4%	2%	100%

162

FOOD	Measure or Weight	Food Energy Cal.	Proteins Gms.	Carbo-hydrates Gms.	Fat Gms.	Choles-terol Mg.	Calcium Mg.	Iron Mg.	Sodium Mg.	Vitamin A IU.	Thiamin Mg.	Ribo-flavin Mg.	Niacin C Mg.	Vitamin C Mg.
Strawberry fruit drink (Hi - C)	6 oz.	98		23	Trace		Trace	Trace	.39	Trace	Trace	Trace	Trace	60
Tangerines, raw, medium 2⅜ in. diam., size 176 (USDA)	1 tangerine	40	1	10	Trace		34	.3		360	.05	.02	.1	27
Tangerine juice, canned, sweetened (USDA)	1 cup	125	1	30	1		45	.5		1050	.15	.05	.2	55
Watermelon, raw, wedge 4 by 8 in. (USDA)	1 wedge	115	2	27	1		30	2.1		2510	.13	.13	.7	30

GRAIN PRODUCTS

GRAIN PRODUCTS

FOOD	Measure or Weight	Food Energy Cal.	Proteins Gms.	Carbo-hydrates Gms.	Fat Gms.	Choles-terol Mg.	Calcium Mg.	Iron Mg.	Sodium Mg.	Vitamin A I.U.	Thiamin Mg.	Ribo-flavin Mg.	Niacin C Mg.	Vitamin C Mg.
BAGELS TO BARLEY														
Bagel, 3-in. diam., egg (USDA)	1 bagel	165	6	28	2		9	1.2	30	30	.14	.1	1.2	0
Bagel, 3-in. diam., water (USDA)	1 bagel	165	6	30	2		8	1.2	0	0	.15	.11	1.4	0
Barley, pearled, light uncooked (USDA)	1 cup	700	16	158	2		32	4	0	0	.24	.1	6.2	0
Barley, pearled, cooked (Quaker Scotch Brand)	1 cup	173	4.6	37.4	.6		11	.8	4	0	.07	.03	1.7	
Barley, pearled, quick cooking, cooked (Quaker Scotch Brand)	¾ cup	173	4.6	37.4	.6		11	.8	4	0	.07	.03	1.7	
BISCUITS														
Baking powder, biscuits, from home recipe with enriched flour, 2 in. diam. (USDA)	1 biscuit	105	2	13	5		34	.4		Trace	.06	.06	.1	Trace

166

FOOD	Measure or Weight	Food Energy Cal.	Proteins Gms.	Carbo-hydrates Gms.	Fat Gms.	Choles-terol Mg.	Calcium Mg.	Iron Mg.	Sodium Mg.	Vitamin A IU.	Thiamin Mg.	Ribo-flavin Mg.	Niacin Mg.	Vitamin C Mg.
Baking powder, biscuits, from mix, 2 in. diam. (USDA)	1 biscuit	90	2	15	3		19	.6		Trace	.08	.07	.6	Trace
Baking powder biscuits, (1869 Brand)	2 biscuits	210	4	26	10		2%	6%	980	0	10%	8%	8%	0
Buttermilk biscuits (Ballard)	2 biscuits	120	3	22	2		0	2%	580	0	10%	6%	6%	0
Buttermilk biscuits (1869 Brand)	2 biscuits	210	4	26	10		2%	6%	610	0	10%	10%	8%	0
Buttermilk biscuits (Pillsbury)	2 biscuits	110	3	21	1		0	2%	1090	0	10%	6%	6%	0
Flaky biscuits (Hungry Jack)	2 biscuits	180	3	23	9		0	4%	1025	0	10%	6%	8%	0
Oven ready biscuits (Ballard)	2 biscuits	120	3	22	2		0	2%	1220	0	10%	6%	6%	0
BRAN CEREALS														
All-bran, wheat bran cereal (Kellogg's)	1 oz.	60	3	20	1		2%	25%		25%	25%	25%	25%	25%

GRAIN PRODUCTS

FOOD	Measure or Weight	Food Energy Cal.	Proteins Gms.	Carbo-hydrates Gms.	Fat Gms.	Choles-terol Mg.	Calcium Mg.	Iron Mg.	Sodium Mg.	Vitamin A IU.	Thiamin Mg.	Ribo-flavin Mg.	Niacin C Mg.	Vitamin C Mg.
Bran flakes, 40% bran, added thiamin and iron (USDA)	1 cup	105	4	28	1		25	12.3		0	.14	.06	2.2	0
Bran flakes, 40% (Kellogg's)	1 oz.	70	3	22	1		★	25%		25%	25%	25%	25%	★
Bran flakes, 40% (Post)	1 oz.	100	2	22	1		★	25%	280	25%	25%	25%	25%	★
Bran buds (Kellogg's)	1 oz.	70	3	21	0		2%	25%		25%	25%	25%	25%	25%
100% Bran cereal (Nabisco)	½ cup	70	3	21	2		2%	15%		★	45%	45%	45%	45%
Total, bran cereal (General Mills)	1 oz.	110	3	23	1		4%	100%		100%	100%	100%	100%	100%
Bran flakes with raisins, added thiamin and iron (USDA)	1 cup	145	4	40	1		28	13.5		Trace	.16	.07	2.7	0
Raisin bran (Kellogg's)	1 oz.	100	3	31	0		2%	25%		25%	25%	25%	2%	★
Raisin Bran (Post)	1 oz.	100	2	22	1		★	25%	195	25%	25%	25%	25%	★

FOOD	Measure or Weight	Food Energy Cal.	Proteins Gms.	Carbohydrates Gms.	Fat Gms.	Cholesterol Mg.	Calcium Mg.	Iron Mg.	Sodium Mg.	Vitamin A IU.	Thiamin Mg.	Riboflavin Mg.	Niacin C Mg.	Vitamin C Mg.
BREADS														
Boston brown bread, slice 3 by ¾ in. (USDA)	1 slice	100	3	22	1		43	.9		0	.05	.03	.6	0
Brown bread, plain (B & M)	1 oz.	52	1.5	11.4	Trace		33.17	.54	139	—	.006	.108	.964	.624
Cracked wheat bread, 18 slices per loaf (USDA)	1 slice	65	2	13	1		22	.3		Trace	.03	.02	.3	Trace
Cracked wheat bread (Wonder)	2 slices	150	5	27	2	0	2%	6%	300	0	10%	6%	8%	0
French or vienna bread, enriched, 1 lb. loaf (USDA)	1 loaf	1315	41	251	14		195	10		Trace	1.27	1	11.3	Trace
French bread (Pepperidge Farm)	2 oz.	150	4	27	2		2%	4%	730	0	8%	4%	8%	0
French bread (Wonder)	2 oz.	150	5	28	2		6%	8%	330	0	15%	8%	10%	0
French toast, frozen (Aunt Jemima)	2 slices	175	6.5	27.2	4.3		67	1.3	440	193	.15	.18	1.1	
French toast, frozen (Eggo)	1 slice	80	3	13	2		2%	10%		10%	10%	10%	10%	★

GRAIN PRODUCTS

FOOD	Measure or Weight	Food Energy Cal.	Proteins Gms.	Carbo-hydrates Gms.	Fat Gms.	Choles-terol Mg.	Calcium Mg.	Iron Mg.	Sodium Mg.	Vitamin A IU.	Thiamin Mg.	Ribo-flavin Mg.	Niacin Mg.	Vitamin C Mg.
French toast with link sausages, frozen breakfast (Swanson)	4½ oz.	300	16	22	17		8%	10%	520	0	20%	20%	10%	0
Italian bread, enriched, 1 lb. loaf (USDA)	1 loaf	1250	41	256	4		77	10		0	1.32	.91	11.8	0
Italian bread (Pepperidge Farm)	2 oz.	140	4	27	3		4%	6%	720	0	10%	6%	8%	0
Pumpernickel, 1 lb. (USDA)	1 loaf	1115	41	241	5		381	10.9		0	1.04	.64	5.4	0
Raisin bread, 18 slices per loaf (USDA)	1 slice	65	2	13	1		18	.3		Trace	.01	.02	.2	Trace
Raisin loaf, cinnamon (Thomas')	1 slice	60	1.7	12.2	.3		15	.6	90		.07	.05	.8	
Raisin rounds (Wonder)	2 oz.	150	4	28	3	0	8%	8%	210	0	15%	10%	8%	0
Rye bread, American, light, 18 slices per loaf (USDA)	1 slice	60	2	13	Trace		19	.4		0	.05	.02	.4	0

FOOD	Measure or Weight	Food Energy Cal.	Proteins Gms.	Carbohydrates Gms.	Fat Gms.	Cholesterol Mg.	Calcium Mg.	Iron Mg.	Sodium Mg.	Vitamin A IU.	Thiamin Mg.	Riboflavin Mg.	Niacin C Mg.	Vitamin C Mg.
Rye bread (Wonder)	2 oz.	150	5	27	2	0	2%	6%	330	0	10%	4%	6%	0
White bread, enriched[15], soft-crumb type, 18 slices per loaf (USDA)	1 slice	70	2	13	1		21	.6		Trace	.06	.05	.6	Trace
White bread, enriched (Wonder)	2 oz.	150	5	27	2	0	6%	8%	330	0	15%	8%	10%	0
White bread, enriched, slice toasted (USDA)	1 slice	70	2	13	1		21	.6		Trace	.06	.05	.6	Trace
White bread, firm-crumb type, 20 slices per loaf (USDA)	1 slice	65	2	12	1		22	.6		Trace	.06	.05	.6	Trace
White bread, large (Pepperidge Farm)	2 slices	150	4	27	3		4%	4%	340	0	8%	6%	8%	0
White bread, sandwich (Pepperidge Farm)	2 slices	120	4	24	2		2%	4%	260	0	6%	4%	6%	0
White bread, very thin, sliced (Pepperidge Farm)	2 slices	90	3	16	1		2%	2%	170	0	4%	2%	4%	0
Wheat bread (Wonder)	2 oz.	150	5	27	2	0	2%	6%	310	0	10%	6%	8%	0

GRAIN PRODUCTS

FOOD	Measure or Weight	Food Energy Cal.	Proteins Gms.	Carbo-hydrates Gms.	Fat Gms.	Choles-terol Mg.	Calcium Mg.	Iron Mg.	Sodium Mg.	Vitamin A IU.	Thiamin Mg.	Ribo-flavin Mg.	Niacin Mg.	Vitamin C Mg.
Whole-wheat bread, soft crumb type, 16 slices per loaf (USDA)	1 slice	65	3	14	1		24	.8		Trace	.09	.03	.8	Trace
Whole-wheat bread, firm crumb type, 18 slices per loaf (USDA)	1 slice	60	3	12	1		25	.8		Trace	.06	.03	.7	Trace
100% whole wheat bread (S.B. Thomas)	1 slice	50	2.1	10.6	.5		10	.6			.08	.05	.8	
Breadcrumbs, dry, grated (USDA)	1 cup	390	13	73	5		122	3.6		Trace	.22	.3	3.5	Trace
Bread mix, banana (Pillsbury)	1/16 loaf	110	2	20	3		0	2%	115	0	6%	4%	2%	0
Bread mix, date (Pillsbury)	1/16 loaf	120	2	23	2		0	4%	110	0	6%	4%	4%	0
Bread mix, nut (Pillsbury)	1/16 loaf	120	2	20	4		0	4%	110	0	6%	4%	2%	0

CAKES — Made from mixes

FOOD	Measure or Weight	Food Energy Cal.	Proteins Gms.	Carbo-hydrates Gms.	Fat Gms.	Choles-terol Mg.	Calcium Mg.	Iron Mg.	Sodium Mg.	Vitamin A IU.	Thiamin Mg.	Ribo-flavin Mg.	Niacin Mg.	Vitamin C Mg.
Angel food, piece, 1/12 of 10 in. diam. cake (USDA)	1 piece	135	3	32	Trace		50	.2		0	Trace	.06	.1	0
Angel food (Duncan Hines)	1/12 cake	130	3	30	0		6%	★		★	★	★	★	★
Angel food (Pillsbury)	1/12 cake	140	3	33	0		2%	0	355	0	2%	6%	0	0
Angel food, one-step (Betty Crocker)	1/12 pkg.	140	3	32	0		4%	★		★	★	6%	★	★
Angel food, traditional (Betty Crocker)	1/12 pkg.	130	3	30	0		4%	★		★	★	6%	★	★
Applesauce raisin (Duncan Hines)	1/9 cake	200	2	37	5		4%	4%		0	4%	4%	4%	0
Applesauce spice layer cake (Pillsbury)	1/12 cake	200	3	34	6		4%	6%	255	2%	8%	8%	4%	0
Banana supreme mix (Duncan Hines)	1/12 cake	200	2	35	6		2%	4%		0	6%	4%	4%	0

173

GRAIN PRODUCTS

FOOD	Measure or Weight	Food Energy Cal.	Proteins Gms.	Carbo-hydrates Gms.	Fat Gms.	Choles-terol Mg.	Calcium Mg.	Iron Mg.	Sodium Mg.	Vitamin A IU.	Thiamin Mg.	Ribo-flavin Mg.	Niacin C Mg.	Vitamin C Mg.
Bundt devil's food (Pillsbury)	1/12 cake	250	4	32	12		0	6%	320	2%	6%	6%	2%	0
Bundt German chocolate (Pillsbury)	1/12 cake	250	3	33	12		0	4%	315	2%	6%	6%	2%	0
Bundt marble supreme (Pillsbury)	1/12 cake	330	4	50	12		2%	6%	340	6%	10%	8%	6%	0
Bundt pound cake (Pillsbury)	1/12 cake	300	4	44	12		2%	6%	350	6%	10%	10%	6%	0
Bundt yellow cake (Pillsbury)	1/12 cake	260	3	33	13		4%	6%	315	2%	6%	6%	4%	0
Butter cake (Pillsbury)	1/12 cake	190	3	32	6		2%	6%	245	2%	8%	8%	4%	0
Butter recipe golden (Duncan Hines)	1/12 cake	280	4	37	14		6%	4%		0	4%	6%	2%	0
Chiffon cake mix, lemon (Betty Crocker)	1/12 cake	190	4	35	4		2%	4%		2%	6%	8%	2%	★

FOOD	Measure or Weight	Food Energy Cal.	Proteins Gms.	Carbohydrates Gms.	Fat Gms.	Cholesterol Mg.	Calcium Mg.	Iron Mg.	Sodium Mg.	Vitamin A IU.	Thiamin Mg.	Riboflavin Mg.	Niacin C Mg.	Vitamin C Mg.
Chocolate fudge (Pillsbury)	1/12 cake	210	3	34	7		0	4%	370	2%	8%	6%	4%	0
Chocolate fudge supreme (Betty Crocker)	1/12 cake	200	3	34	6		4%	4%		2%	4%	4%	4%	★
Coffee cake, easy mix (Aunt Jemima)	⅛ cake	186	3	30.3	5.8		70	.74	211	95	.08	.08	.7	
Coffee cake mix, butter pecan (Pillsbury)	⅛ cake	310	4	39	15		4%	4%	335	8%	10%	8%	4%	0
Coffee cake mix, cinnamon streusel (Pillsbury)	⅛ cake	250	3	41	8		4%	6%	225	2%	8%	6%	4%	0
Cupcakes, 2½ in. diam., without icing (USDA)	1 cupcake	90	1	14	3		40	.1		40	.01	.03	.1	Trace
Cupcakes, 2½ in., with chocolate icing (USDA)	1 cupcake	130	2	21	5		47	.3		60	.01	.04	.1	Trace
Cupcake mix (Flako)	1 cupcake	140	1.9	21.9	5		54	.4			.05	.06	.4	
Devil's food, 2 layer cake with chocolate icing, 1/16 of 9 in. diam. cake (USDA)	1 piece	235	3	40	9		41	.6		100	.02	.06	.2	Trace

GRAIN PRODUCTS

FOOD	Measure or Weight	Food Energy Cal.	Proteins Gms.	Carbo-hydrates Gms.	Fat Gms.	Choles-terol Mg.	Calcium Mg.	Iron Mg.	Sodium Mg.	Vitamin A IU.	Thiamin Mg.	Ribo-flavin Mg.	Niacin C Mg.	Vitamin C Mg.
Devil's food (Betty Crocker)	1/12 cake	200	3	34	6		6%	4%		2%	4%	4%	4%	★
Devil's food (Duncan Hines)	1/12 cake	200	3	35	7		2%	6%		0	0	6%	4%	0
Fruit 'N Crunch bar mix, apple (Pillsbury)	2" square	140	1	18	7		2%	2%	180	4%	4%	2%	2%	0
Fruit 'N Crunch bar mix, cherry (Pillsbury)	2" square	150	2	20	7		2%	2%	180	4%	4%	2%	2%	0
Fudge marble cake mix (Duncan Hines)	1/12 cake	200	3	35	6		4%	6%		0	4%	6%	4%	0
German chocolate (Betty Crocker)	1/12 cake	200	3	34	6		4%	4%		2%	6%	4%	4%	★
German chocolate layer cake (Pillsbury)	1/12 cake	210	3	35	7		2%	6%	340	2%	8%	6%	4%	0
Gingerbread, 1/9 of 8 in. square cake (USDA)	1 piece	175	2	32	4		57	1		Trace	.02	.06	.5	Trace
Gingerbread (Pillsbury)	3 in. sq.	190	2	36	4		4%	8%	340	0	8%	6%	6%	0

FOOD	Measure or Weight	Food Energy Cal.	Proteins Gms.	Carbohydrates Gms.	Fat Gms.	Cholesterol Mg.	Calcium Mg.	Iron Mg.	Sodium Mg.	Vitamin A IU.	Thiamin Mg.	Riboflavin Mg.	Niacin C Mg.	Vitamin C Mg.
Lemon cake (Pillsbury)	1/12 cake	200	3	33	6		2%	6%	250	2%	8%	8%	4%	0
Lemon supreme cake (Duncan Hines)	1/12 cake	200	3	35	6		4%	4%		0	6%	4%	4%	0
Marble cake mix (Betty Crocker)	1/12 cake	200	3	34	6		10%	4%		2%	6%	4%	4%	★
Orange supreme (Duncan Hines)	1/12 cake	200	3	35	6		4%	4%		0	6%	4%	4%	0
Pudding cake mix, chocolate (Betty Crocker)	1/6 pkg. prepared	230	2	45	5		4%	4%		2%	4%	6%	2%	★
Snack cake mix, banana nut (Duncan Hines)	1/9 cake	190	2	31	6		4%	4%	230	★	★	4%	4%	★
Snack cake, double choc. chip (Duncan Hines)	1/9 cake	180	3	32	5		6%	6%	340	★	★	4%	4%	★
Snack cake, spicy apple raisin (Duncan Hines)	1/9 cake	180	2	33	4		2%	2%	240	★	★	4%	4%	★
Snackin' cake mix, choc. chip (Betty Crocker)	1/9 pkg.	220	3	35	7		2%	4%		★	8%	6%	4%	★

GRAIN PRODUCTS

FOOD	Measure or Weight	Food Energy Cal.	Proteins Gms.	Carbo-hydrates Gms.	Fat Gms.	Choles-terol Mg.	Calcium Mg.	Iron Mg.	Sodium Mg.	Vitamin A IU.	Thiamin Mg.	Ribo-flavin Mg.	Niacin C Mg.	Vitamin C Mg.
Snackin' mix, spice raisin (Betty Crocker)	1/9 pkg.	200	3	34	6		2%	4%		★	6%	6%	4%	★
Sour cream white cake (Betty Crocker)	1/12 cake	200	3	34	6		10%	4%		2%	6%	4%	4%	★
Sour cream yellow cake (Betty Crocker)	1/12 cake	200	3	34	6		8%	4%		2%	6%	4%	4%	★
Spicecake (Duncan Hines)	1/12 cake	200	3	35	6		6%	4%		0	4%	4%	4%	0
Streusel swirl, devil's food (Pillsbury)	1/12 cake	330	4	47	14		4%	6%	460	2%	8%	8%	4%	0
Streusel swirl, lemon (Pillsbury)	1/12 cake	340	4	49	14		8%	6%	395	2%	10%	8%	4%	0
Streusel swirl, spice (Pillsbury)	1/12 cake	350	4	48	16		10%	8%	380	2%	8%	6%	4%	0
Sunkist lemon (Betty Crocker)	1/12 cake	200	3	34	6		10%	2%		2%	8%	4%	4%	★

FOOD	Measure or Weight	Food Energy Cal.	Proteins Gms.	Carbohydrates Gms.	Fat Gms.	Cholesterol Mg.	Calcium Mg.	Iron Mg.	Sodium Mg.	Vitamin A IU.	Thiamin Mg.	Riboflavin Mg.	Niacin C Mg.	Vitamin C Mg.
Sunkist orange (Betty Crocker)	1/12 cake	200	3	34	6		8%	2%		2%	6%	4%	4%	★
White cake mix (Betty Crocker)	1/12 cake	200	3	35	5		4%	2%		★	6%	4%	4%	★
White cake mix (Duncan Hines)	1/12 cake	190	2	36	4		2%	2%		0	6%	4%	4%	0
White cake mix (Pillsbury)	1/12 cake	200	2	35	6		2%	4%	255	0	8%	8%	4%	0
White 2-layer cake with chocolate icing, 1/16 of 9 in. diam. cake (USDA)	1 piece	250	3	45	8		70	.4		40	.01	.06	.1	Trace
Yellow cake mix (Betty Crocker)	1/12 cake	190	2	34	5		6%	4%		2%	6%	4%	4%	★
Yellow cake (Duncan Hines)	1/12 cake	200	3	35	6		4%	4%		0	6%	4%	4%	0
Yellow cake (Pillsbury)	1/12 cake	200	3	33	6		2%	6%	250	2%	8%	8%	4%	0

GRAIN PRODUCTS

— Made from home recipes[16]

FOOD	Measure or Weight	Food Energy Cal.	Proteins Gms.	Carbo-hydrates Gms.	Fat Gms.	Choles-terol Mg.	Calcium Mg.	Iron Mg.	Sodium Mg.	Vitamin A IU.	Thiamin Mg.	Ribo-flavin Mg.	Niacin C Mg.	Vitamin C Mg.
Boston cream pie; piece 1/12 of 8 in. diam. (USDA)	1 piece	210	4	34	6		46	.3		140	.02	.08	.1	Trace
Fruitcake, dark, made with enriched flour, slice 1/30 of 8 in. loaf (USDA)	1 slice	55	1	9	2		11	.4		20	.02	.02	.1	Trace
Plain sheet cake without icing, piece 1/9 of 9 in. square cake (USDA)	1 piece	315	4	48	12		55	.3		150	.02	.08	.2	Trace
Plain sheet cake with boiled white icing, piece 1/9 of 9 in. square cake (USDA)	1 piece	400	4	71	12		56	.3		150	.02	.08	.2	Trace
Pound cake, slice ½ in. thick (USDA)	1 slice	140	2	14	9		6	.2		80	.01	.03	.1	0
Sponge cake, piece 1/12 of 10 in. diam. cake (USDA)	1 piece	195	5	36	4		20	.8		300	.03	.09	.1	Trace

FOOD	Measure or Weight	Food Energy Cal.	Proteins Gms.	Carbo-hydrates Gms.	Fat Gms.	Choles-terol Mg.	Calcium Mg.	Iron Mg.	Sodium Mg.	Vitamin A IU.	Thiamin Mg.	Ribo-flavin Mg.	Niacin C Mg.	Vitamin C Mg.
Yellow, 2-layer without icing, piece 1/16 of 9 in. diam. cake (USDA)	1 piece	200	2	32	7		39	.2		80	.01	.04	.1	Trace
Yellow, 2-layer cake with chocolate icing, piece 1/16 of 9 in. diam. cake (USDA)	1 piece	275	3	45	10		51	.5		120	.02	.06	.2	Trace
— Commercial														
Cupcakes, devil's food (Hostess)	1 cake	160	1	26	5	5	2%	8%	250	0	6%	4%	4%	0
Cupcakes, orange (Hostess)	1 cake	170	1	26	7	10	2%	6%	170	0	6%	6%	4%	0
Twinkies, devil's food (Hostess)	1 cake	170	1	27	7	20	2%	6%	220	0	4%	6%	4%	0
Twinkies, golden sponge (Hostess)	2 cakes	320	2	52	11	40	2%	8%	380	0	15%	4%	4%	0
COOKIES														
Arrowroot (Sunshine)	1 biscuit	16	.2	3	.4		1.4	.09						

181

GRAIN PRODUCTS

FOOD	Measure or Weight	Food Energy Cal.	Proteins Gms.	Carbo-hydrates Gms.	Fat Gms.	Choles-terol Mg.	Calcium Mg.	Iron Mg.	Sodium Mg.	Vitamin A IU.	Thiamin Mg.	Ribo-flavin Mg.	Niacin C Mg.	Vitamin C Mg.
Brownies with nuts from home recipe with enriched flour (USDA)	1 brownie	95	1	10	6		8	.4		40	.04	.02	.1	Trace
Brownies made from mix (USDA)	1 brownie	85	1	13	4		9	.4		20	.03	.02	.1	Trace
Brownies (Duncan Hines)	1 brownie	150	2	20	7		0	2%		0	2%	4%	2%	0
Brownies, fudge (Pillsbury)	2 squares	120	1	19	4		0	2%	105	0	2%	2%	0	0
Butterscotch nut cookies (Pillsbury)	3 cookies	120	1	16	6		2%	0	140	0	4%	2%	2%	0
Chocolate chip, made from home recipe with enriched flour (USDA)	1 cookie	50	1	6	3		4	.2		10	.01	.01	.1	Trace
Chocolate chip, commercial, (USDA)	1 cookie	50	1	7	2		4	.2		10	Trace	Trace	Trace	Trace
Chocolate chip, Chips Ahoy (Nabisco)	3 cookies	160	2	22	7		★	4%		★	4%	6%	2%	★

FOOD	Measure or Weight	Food Energy Cal.	Proteins Gms.	Carbo-hydrates Gms.	Fat Gms.	Choles-terol Mg.	Calcium Mg.	Iron Mg.	Sodium Mg.	Vitamin A IU.	Thiamin Mg.	Ribo-flavin Mg.	Niacin C Mg.	Vitamin C Mg.
Chocolate chip (Pillsbury)	3 cookies	130	1	19	6		0	0	105	0	2%	2%	2%	0
Chocolate Chip, Chip-A-Roos (Sunshine)	1 biscuit	63	.6	7.7	2.9		2.7	.24						
Chocolate chip, coconut (Sunshine)	1 biscuit	80	.8	9.7	4.3		7.5	.34						
Fig bars, commercial (USDA)	1 cookie	50	1	11	1		11	.2		20	Trace	.01	.1	Trace
Fig Newtons (Nabisco)	2 bars	110	1	23	2		★	4%		★	★	4%	2%	★
Golden fruit (Sunshine)	1 biscuit	61	.7	14.4	.6		12.6	.62						
Iced oatmeal (Sunshine)	1 biscuit	69	.8	11.6	2.2		2.9	.29						
Lemon cookies (Sunshine)	1 biscuit	76	.9	9.8	3.7		5.9	.3						
Lorna Doone shortbread (Nabisco)	4 cookies	160	2	19	8		★	4%		★	4%	4%	2%	★
Mallopuffs (Sunshine)	1 biscuit	63	.5	12.2	1.6		2.2	.16						
Oatmeal cookies (Sunshine)	1 biscuit	58	.7	1.5	2.3		2.8	.29						

GRAIN PRODUCTS

FOOD	Measure or Weight	Food Energy Cal.	Proteins Gms.	Carbo-hydrates Gms.	Fat Gms.	Choles-terol Mg.	Calcium Mg.	Iron Mg.	Sodium Mg.	Vitamin A IU.	Thiamin Mg.	Ribo-flavin Mg.	Niacin C Mg.	Vitamin C Mg.
Oatmeal chocolate chip (Pillsbury)	3 cookies	130	1	18	6		0	0	55	0	2%	2%	0	0
Oatmeal raisin (Pillsbury)	3 cookies	140	1	20	6		0	2%	75	0	4%	0	2%	0
Peanut butter cookie (Pillsbury)	3 cookies	130	2	15	7		2%	0	180	0	4%	2%	6%	0
Sandwich, chocolate or vanilla, commercial (USDA)	1 cookie	50	1	7	2		2	.1		0	Trace	Trace	.1	0
Hydrox (Sunshine)	1 biscuit	48	.4	7.1	2.2		1.4	.21						
Oreo chocolate sandwich cookies (Nabisco)	3	150	1	22	6		★	4%		★	2%	2%	★	★
Social tea biscuit (Nabisco)	6 biscuits	120	2	21	3		★	4%		★	2%	4%	4%	★
Sugar cookie (Pillsbury)	3 cookies	130	1	19	6		2%	0	170	0	6%	2%	2%	0
Sugar cookie (Sunshine)	1 biscuit	86	1	11.9	3.7		2.2	.38						

FOOD	Measure or Weight	Food Energy Cal.	Proteins Gms.	Carbohydrates Gms.	Fat Gms.	Cholesterol Mg.	Calcium Mg.	Iron Mg.	Sodium Mg.	Vitamin A IU.	Thiamin Mg.	Riboflavin Mg.	Niacin C Mg.	Vitamin C Mg.
Sugar wafers, Biscos (Nabisco)	8 wafers	150	1	20	7		★	2%		★	★	2%	2%	★
Sugar wafers (Sunshine)	1 biscuit	43	.3	6.6	1.8		5	.1						
Toy cookies (Sunshine)	1 biscuit	13	.2	2.1	.4		2.9	.07						
Vanilla wafers (Nabisco)	7 wafers	130	1	21	4		★	2%		★	2%	4%	2%	★
Vanilla wafers, small (Sunshine)	1 biscuit	15	.2	2.2	.6		.6	.07						
Vienna finger sandwich (Sunshine)	1 biscuit	71	.7	10.5	2.9		5.4	.29						
CORN PRODUCTS - Bread														
Corn bread, easy mix (Aunt Jemima)	1/6 recipe	228	5.1	34.9	7.6		40	1	575		.12	.13	.8	
Corn bread mix (Ballard)	1/8 recipe	160	4	26	4		4%	6%	720	2%	10%	10%	6%	0
— Cereals														
Cocoa Puffs (General Mills)	1 oz.	110	1	25	1		★	25%		★	25%	25%	25%	25%

GRAIN PRODUCTS

FOOD	Measure or Weight	Food Energy Cal.	Proteins Gms.	Carbohydrates Gms.	Fat Gms.	Cholesterol Mg.	Calcium Mg.	Iron Mg.	Sodium Mg.	Vitamin A IU.	Thiamin Mg.	Riboflavin Mg.	Niacin C Mg.	Vitamin C Mg.
Corn flakes, added nutrients, plain (USDA)	1 cup	100	2	21	Trace		4			0	.11	.02	.5	0
Corn flakes (Kellogg's)	1 oz.	110	2	25	0		★	10%		25%	25%	25%	25%	25%
Corn flakes, sugar-covered (USDA)	1 cup	155	2	36	Trace		5	.4		0	.16	.02	.8	0
Corn Total (General Mills)	1 oz.	110	2	24	1		4%	100%		100%	100%	100%	100%	100%
Country corn flakes (General Mills)	1 oz.	110	2	24	1		★	25%		25%	25%	25%	25%	25%
Golden Grahams corn cereal (General Mills)	1 oz.	110	2	24	1		2%	25%		25%	25%	25%	25%	25%
Honeycomb crisp sweetened corn cereal (Post)	1 oz.	110	1	25	0		★	2%	235	25%	25%	25%	25%	★
Kix corn cereal (General Mills)	1 oz.	110	2	24	1		★	25%		25%	25%	25%	25%	25%
Post Toasties (Post)	1 oz.	110	2	24	0		★	2%	325	25%	25%	25%	25%	★

FOOD	Measure or Weight	Food Energy Cal.	Proteins Gms.	Carbo-hydrates Gms.	Fat Gms.	Choles-terol Mg.	Calcium Mg.	Iron Mg.	Sodium Mg.	Vitamin A IU.	Thiamin Mg.	Ribo-flavin Mg.	Niacin C Mg.	Vitamin C Mg.
Sugar frosted corn flakes (Kellogg's)	1 oz.	110	1	26	0		★	10%		25%	25%	25%	25%	25%
Sugar pops, puffed corn (Kellogg's)	1 oz.	110	1	26	0		★	10%		25%	25%	25%	25%	25%
Trix corn cereal (General Mills)	1 oz.	110	1	25	1		★	25%		25%	25%	25%	25%	25%
— Grits to Starch														
Corn hominy grits, degermed, cooked, enriched (USDA)	1 cup	125	3	27	Trace		2	.7		150[17]	.1	.07	1	0
Corn hominy grits, cooked, enriched (Quaker or Aunt Jemima)	⅔ cup	100	2.4	22	.2		3	.8	.9		.12	.07	1	
Corn hominy grits, unenriched (USDA)	1 cup	125	3	27	Trace		2	.2		150[17]	.05	.02	.5	0
Corn hominy grits, product, instant (Quaker)	1 packet	78	1.9	17.5	.1		2	.65	347		.1	.06	.8	
Cornflake crumbs (Kellogg's)	1 oz.	110	2	25	0		★	10%		25%	25%	25%	25%	25%

GRAIN PRODUCTS

FOOD	Measure or Weight	Food Energy Cal.	Proteins Gms.	Carbohydrates Gms.	Fat Gms.	Cholesterol Mg.	Calcium Mg.	Iron Mg.	Sodium Mg.	Vitamin A IU.	Thiamin Mg.	Riboflavin Mg.	Niacin C Mg.	Vitamin C Mg.
Cornmeal, degermed, enriched, cooked (USDA)	1 cup	120	3	26	1		2	1		140_{17}	.14	.10	1.2	0
Cornmeal, enriched, uncooked bolted (Quaker or Aunt Jemima)	¼ cup	102	2.3	21.2	.9		2	.8	.2		.12	.07	1	
Cornmeal, enriched, uncooked, degerminated (Quaker or Aunt Jemima)	¼ cup	101	2.1	22.2	.4		1	.8	.2		.12	.07	1	
Corn muffins, made with enriched, degermed cornmeal and enriched flour; 2⅜ in. diam. (USDA)	1 muffin	125	3	19	4		42	.7		120_{17}	.08	.09	.6	Trace
Corn muffins, made with mix, egg and milk; 2⅜ in. diam. (USDA)	1 muffin	130	3	20	4		96	.6		100	.07	.08	.6	Trace
Corn muffin mix (Flako)	1 muffin	133	2.7	20.7	4.3		32	.4	295		.05	.06	.5	
Corn muffins (S.B. Thomas)	1 muffin	185	3.5	25.9	7.2		35	1.6	330		.14	.11	.1	

FOOD	Measure or Weight	Food Energy Cal.	Proteins Gms.	Carbo-hydrates Gms.	Fat Gms.	Choles-terol Mg.	Calcium Mg.	Iron Mg.	Sodium Mg.	Vitamin A IU.	Thiamin Mg.	Ribo-flavin Mg.	Niacin C Mg.	Vitamin C Mg.
Corn muffins, frozen, 10 oz. (Morton)	1.66 oz.	130	3	20	5		2%	2%	280	2%	4%	4%	2%	0
Corn muffin rounds, frozen 9 oz. (Morton)	1.5 oz.	130	2	20	4		0	2%	170	0	4%	4%	2%	0
Corn starch (Argo Kingsford/Duryea's)	1 tbsp.	35	0	8	0		★	★	<5	★	★	★	★	★
CRACKERS														
Cheese Nips crackers (Nabisco)	26 crackers	150	2	18	7		2%	4%		★	6%	6%	4%	★
Cheez-its (Sunshine)	1 biscuit	6	.1	.6	.3		1.4	.03						
Escort crackers (Nabisco)	7 crackers	150	2	19	7		★	4%		★	6%	6%	2%	★
Graham, 2½ in. square (USDA)	4 crackers	110	2	21	3		.4	0		0	.01	.06	.4	0
Honey Maid graham crackers (Nabisco)	4 crackers	120	2	22	3		★	4%		★	★	8%	4%	★
Krispy crackers (Sunshine)	1 biscuit	11	.2	2	.2		.8	.1						

GRAIN PRODUCTS

FOOD	Measure or Weight	Food Energy Cal.	Proteins Gms.	Carbo-hydrates Gms.	Fat Gms.	Choles-terol Mg.	Calcium Mg.	Iron Mg.	Sodium Mg.	Vitamin A IU.	Thiamin Mg.	Ribo-flavin Mg.	Niacin C Mg.	Vitamin C Mg.
Oysters, mini cracker (Sunshine)	1 biscuit	3	.1	.6	.1		.2	.03						
Ritz crackers (Nabisco)	9 crackers	150	2	18	8		4%	4%		★	4%	4%	4%	★
Rye wafers, whole grain, 1⅞ by 3½ in. (USDA)	2 wafers	45	2	10	Trace		7	.5		0	.04	.03	.2	0
Saltines (USDA)	4 crackers	50	1	8	1		2	.1		0	Trace	Trace	.1	0
Saltine crackers, Premium (Nabisco)	10 crackers	120	2	20	3		4%	6%		★	8%	6%	4%	★
Soda crackers (Sunshine)	1 biscuit	20	.4	3.3	.5		1	.17						
Triscuit wafers (Nabisco)	7 wafers	140	3	21	5		★	4%		2%	2%	2%	6%	★
Wheat thins crackers (Nabisco)	16 crackers	140	2	19	6		★	6%		★	8%	6%	6%	★

FOOD	Measure or Weight	Food Energy Cal.	Proteins Gms.	Carbo-hydrates Gms.	Fat Gms.	Choles-terol Mg.	Calcium Mg.	Iron Mg.	Sodium Mg.	Vitamin A IU.	Thiamin Mg.	Ribo-flavin Mg.	Niacin C Mg.	Vitamin C Mg.
DOUGHNUTS														
Doughnuts, cake type (USDA)	1 doughnut	125	1	16	6		13	.4[18]		30	.05[18]	.05[18]	.4[18]	Trace
Chocolate iced donuts, frozen (Morton)	1.5 oz.	150	2	19	7	10	0	4%	75	0	6%	4%	4%	0
Jelly donuts, frozen (Morton)	1.83 oz.	180	3	22	8	10	2%	4%	75	0	6%	4%	4%	0
Plain cake donuts, frozen (Morton)	1.71 oz.	170	4	23	7	30	2%	4%	90	2%	8%	6%	4%	0
Powdered cake donuts, frozen (Morton)	1.87 oz.	190	4	28	7	30	2%	4%	90	2%	8%	4%	4%	0
FLOUR														
All-purpose or family flour, enriched, sifted (USDA)	1 cup	420	12	88	1		18	3.3[19]		0	.51[9]	.3[19]	4[19]	0
All-purpose or family flour, enriched, unsifted (USDA)	1 cup	455	13	95	1		20	3.6[19]		0	.55[19]	.33[19]	4.4[19]	0

GRAIN PRODUCTS

FOOD	Measure or Weight	Food Energy Cal.	Proteins Gms.	Carbohydrates Gms.	Fat Gms.	Cholesterol Mg.	Calcium Mg.	Iron Mg.	Sodium Mg.	Vitamin A IU.	Thiamin Mg.	Riboflavin Mg.	Niacin C Mg.	Vitamin C Mg.
All-purpose flour (Pillsbury)	1 cup	400	11	87	1		0	15%	<5	0	45%	25%	30%	0
Buckwheat flour, light, sifted (USDA)	1 cup	340	6	78	1		11	1		0	.08	.04	.4	0
Cake or pastry flour, sifted (USDA)	1 cup	350	7	76	1		16	.5		0	.03	.03	.7	0
Plain flour (Ballard)	1 cup	400	10	87	1		0	15%	<5	0	45%	25%	30%	0
Self-rising, enriched (USDA)	1 cup	440	12	93	1		331	3.6_{19}		0	$.55_{19}$	$.33_{19}$	4.4_{19}	0
Self-rising, enriched (Aunt Jemima)	1/4 cup	96	2.4	20.8	.3		31	.8	350	0	.12	.07	1	
Self-rising flour (Ballard)	1 cup	380	10	84	1		20%	15%	1225	0	45%	25%	30%	0
Self-rising flour (Pillsbury)	1 cup	380	10	84	1		20%	15%	1225	0	45%	25%	30%	0
Self-rising cake flour (Presto)	1/4 cup	100	2	21	0	0	★	★	340	★	★	★	★	★

FOOD	Measure or Weight	Food Energy Cal.	Proteins Gms.	Carbo-hydrates Gms.	Fat Gms.	Choles-terol Mg.	Calcium Mg.	Iron Mg.	Sodium Mg.	Vitamin A IU.	Thiamin Mg.	Ribo-flavin Mg.	Niacin C Mg.	Vitamin C Mg.
Whole wheat, flour from hard wheats, stirred (USDA)	1 cup	400	16	85	2		49	4		0	.66	.14	5.2	0
Whole wheat flour (Pillsbury)	1 cup	400	16	80	2		4%	20%	<5	0	40%	8%	25%	0
MACARONI														
Macaroni, enriched, cooked firm (USDA)	1 cup	190	6	39	1		14	1.4[19]		0	.23[19]	.14[19]	1.8[19]	0
Macaroni, enriched, cooked until tender (USDA)	1 cup	155	5	32	1		8	1.3[19]		0	.20[19]	.11[19]	1.5[19]	0
Macaroni, enriched (San Giorgio)	2 oz. dry	210	7	42	1		★	10%		★	30%	10%	15%	★
Macaroni, unenriched, cooked firm (USDA)	1 cup	190	6	39	1		14	.7		0	.03	.03	.5	0
Macaroni, unenriched, cooked until tender (USDA)	1 cup	155	5	32	1		11	.6		0	.01	.01	.4	0

GRAIN PRODUCTS

FOOD	Measure or Weight	Food Energy Cal.	Proteins Gms.	Carbo-hydrates Gms.	Fat Gms.	Choles-terol Mg.	Calcium Mg.	Iron Mg.	Sodium Mg.	Vitamin A IU.	Thiamin Mg.	Ribo-flavin Mg.	Niacin C Mg.	Vitamin C Mg.
Macaroni 'n beef in tomato sauce, canned (Franco - American)	7½ oz.	220	8	27	9		2%	10%	1235	10%	10%	10%	15%	2%
Macaroni & beef dinner, frozen (Banquet)	12 oz.	394	12.6	55.1	13.6		75	3.4	2254	7014	.37	.24	4.01	21.4
Macaroni and beef dinner, frozen (Morton)	11 oz.	310	11	47	9	20	4%	15%	790	90%	15%	10%	15%	50%
Macaroni and beef dinner, frozen (Swanson)	12 oz.	400	12	56	15	51	15%	15%	310	15%	10%	15%	15%	4%
Macaroni & cheddar casserole mix (Betty Crocker)	¼ package	220	9	35	5		20%	6%		★	25%	15%	10%	★
Macaroni and cheese, enriched, baked (USDA)	1 cup	430	17	40	22		362	1.8		860	.2	.4	1.8	Trace
Macaroni and cheese (Pennsylvania Dutch)	½ cup	150	6	24	3		6%	4%		★	15%	10%	8%	★
Macaroni and cheese, canned (USDA)	1 cup	230	9	26	9		199	1		260	.12	.24	1	Trace

FOOD	Measure or Weight	Food Energy Cal.	Proteins Gms.	Carbo-hydrates Gms.	Fat Gms.	Choles-terol Mg.	Calcium Mg.	Iron Mg.	Sodium Mg.	Vitamin A IU.	Thiamin Mg.	Ribo-flavin Mg.	Niacin C Mg.	Vitamin C Mg.
Macaroni and cheese, canned (Franco - American)	7¼ oz.	200	8	26	8		10%	8%	885	10%	10%	10%	10%	0
Macaroni and cheese dinner, frozen (Banquet)	12 oz.	340	13.3	45.6	10.2		224	6.1	1768	5977	.34	.27	2.48	21.4
Macaroni and cheese dinner, frozen (Morton)	11 oz.	350	11	52	11	20	20%	10%	895	80%	15%	15%	8%	30%
Macaroni and cheese dinner, frozen (Swanson)	12½ oz.	390	12	55	14	24	20%	8%	1065	100%	10%	20%	6%	0
Macaroni and cheese meat pie, frozen (Swanson)	1 pie	230	8	26	10		10%	8%	655	10%	10%	8%	6%	0
MUFFINS														
Muffins, with enriched white flour, 3 in. diam. (USDA)	1 muffin	120	3	17	4		42	.6		40	.07	.09	.6	Trace
Muffins, English (S.B. Thomas)	1 muffin	130	4.2	26.8	.6		35	1.3	215		.21	.13	1.66	
Muffins, English (Wonder)	2 oz.	130	4	26	1	0	8%	8%	250	0	15%	8%	10%	0

GRAIN PRODUCTS

FOOD	Measure or Weight	Food Energy Cal.	Proteins Gms.	Carbo-hydrates Gms.	Fat Gms.	Choles-terol Mg.	Calcium Mg.	Iron Mg.	Sodium Mg.	Vitamin A IU.	Thiamin Mg.	Ribo-flavin Mg.	Niacin C Mg.	Vitamin C Mg.
Muffins, English, onion (S.B. Thomas)	1 muffin	135	4.2	26.8	.7		35	1.3	205		.21	.13	1.66	
Muffins, sour dough (Wonder)	2 oz.	130	4	27	1	0	8%	8%	250	0	15%	8%	10%	0
Muffins, wheat berry (Wonder)	2 oz.	130	4	27	1	0	8%	10%	250	0	15%	10%	10%	0
Muffin mix (Duncan Hines)	1 muffin	90	1	16	3		2%	2%		0	2%	2%	2%	0
Muffins, blueberry, frozen (Morton)	1.58 oz.	120	2	22	3	10	0	2%	130	0	4%	4%	2%	0
NOODLES														
Noodles, egg, cooked, enriched (USDA)	1 cup	200	7	37	2		16	1.4[19]		110	.22[19]	.13[19]	1.9[19]	0
Egg noodles, fine, medium, broad (Pennsylvania Dutch Brand)	2 oz.	210	7	40	3		★	8%		★	30%	10%	15%	★

FOOD	Measure or Weight	Food Energy Cal.	Proteins Gms.	Carbohydrates Gms.	Fat Gms.	Cholesterol Mg.	Calcium Mg.	Iron Mg.	Sodium Mg.	Vitamin A IU.	Thiamin Mg.	Riboflavin Mg.	Niacin C Mg.	Vitamin C Mg.
Egg noodles plus beef sauce (Pennsylvania Dutch Brand) ½ cup		140	5	24	2		*	4%		*	15%	6%	8%	*
Egg noodles plus butter sauce (Pennsylvania Dutch Brand) ½ cup		150	4	23	5		2%	4%		*	15%	8%	8%	*
Egg noodles plus cheese sauce (Pennsylvania Dutch Brand) ½ cup		150	5	24	3		4%	4%		*	15%	8%	8%	*
Noodles, enriched (San Giorgio)	2 oz.	220	8	40	3		2%	10%		*	30%	10%	15%	*
Noodles Almondine (Betty Crocker)	¼ pkg.	180	6	25	6		4%	6%		*	15%	10%	10%	*
Noodles Romanoff (Betty Crocker)	¼ pkg.	160	7	22	5		8%	4%		*	15%	6%	8%	*
OAT CEREALS														
Oats, with or without corn, puffed, added nutrients (USDA)	1 cup	100	3	19	1		44	1.2		0	.24	.04	.5	0

GRAIN PRODUCTS

FOOD	Measure or Weight	Food Energy Cal.	Proteins Gms.	Carbo-hydrates Gms.	Fat Gms.	Choles-terol Mg.	Calcium Mg.	Iron Mg.	Sodium Mg.	Vitamin A IU.	Thiamin Mg.	Ribo-flavin Mg.	Niacin C Mg.	Vitamin C Mg.
Alpha-Bits (Post)	1 cup	110	2	24	1		★	4%	210	25%	25%	25%	25%	★
Cheerios, oat cereal (General Mills)	1 oz.	110	4	20	2		4%	25%		25%	25%	25%	25%	25%
Frosty O's (General Mills)	1 oz.	110	2	24	1		2%	25%		25%	25%	25%	25%	25%
Lucky Charms (General Mills)	1 oz.	110	2	24	1		2%	25%		25%	25%	25%	25%	25%
Nature Valley Granola, cinnamon & raisin, (General Mills)	1 oz.	130	3	19	5		2%	6%		★	6%	2%	★	★
Oat flakes, fortified (Post)	1 oz.	110	5	20	1		4%	25%	315	25%	25%	25%	25%	★
Oatmeal or rolled oats, cooked (USDA)	1 cup	130	5	23	2		22	1.4		0	.19	.05	.2	0
Old fashioned oats (H - O)	½ cup dry	140	6	24	2	0	★	8%	<5	★	10%	2%	★	★
Oats, quick or old fashioned (Quaker)	⅓ cup uncooked	107	4.1	18.8	1.7		14	1	1		.15	.03	.2	

FOOD	Measure or Weight	Food Energy Cal.	Proteins Gms.	Carbo-hydrates Gms.	Fat Gms.	Choles-terol Mg.	Calcium Mg.	Iron Mg.	Sodium Mg.	Vitamin A IU.	Thiamin Mg.	Ribo-flavin Mg.	Niacin C Mg.	Vitamin C Mg.
Instant oatmeal (H - 0)	½ cup dry	130	5	23	2	0	★	8%	<5	★	8%	2%	★	★
Quick oats (H - 0)	½ cup dry	130	5	23	2	0	★	6%	<5	★	10%	2%	★	★
PANCAKES														
Pancakes, 4 in. diam., wheat enriched flour, home recipe (USDA)	1 cake	60	2	9	2		27	.4		30	.05	.06	.4	Trace
Pancake and waffle mix, 4 in. diam. pancakes (Aunt Jemima Original)	3 pancakes	181	6	23.5	6.9		186	1.16	450	215	.15	.16	.7	
Blueberry pancake mix, 4 in. diam., pancakes (Hungry Jack)	3 pancakes	340	1	43	16		10%	6%	925	4%	15%	15%	8%	0
Buckwheat pancakes, made from mix with egg and milk (USDA)	1 cake	55	2	6	2		59	.4		60	.03	.04	.2	Trace
Buckwheat pancake and waffle mix, 4 in. diam., pancakes (Aunt Jemima)	3 pancakes	183	6.8	22.5	7.2		193	1.31	444	215	.16	.17	1.2	

GRAIN PRODUCTS

FOOD	Measure or Weight	Food Energy Cal.	Proteins Gms.	Carbo-hydrates Gms.	Fat Gms.	Choles-terol Mg.	Calcium Mg.	Iron Mg.	Sodium Mg.	Vitamin A IU.	Thiamin Mg.	Ribo-flavin Mg.	Niacin C Mg.	Vitamin C Mg.
Buttermilk or plain, made from mix with egg and milk (USDA)	1 cake	60	2	9	2		58	.3		70	.04	.06	.2	Trace
Buttermilk pancake and waffle mix, 4 in. diam., pancakes (Aunt Jemima)	3 pancakes	251	8.6	33.7	9		254	1.88	735	282	.23	.24	1.6	
Buttermilk pancake mix, 4 in. diam., pancakes (Hungry Jack)	3 pancakes	240	7	29	11		6%	6%	570	4%	15%	20%	10%	0
Pancake and link sausage breakfast, frozen (Swanson)	1 breakfast	500	15	50	25		6%	6%	1050	0	20%	15%	10%	0
PASTRY														
Danish pastry, plain, round piece, approx. 4¼ in. diam. by 1 in. (USDA)	1 pastry	275	5	30	15		33	.6		200	.05	.1	.5	Trace
	1 oz.	120	2	13	7		14	.3		90	.02	.04	.2	Trace

PIES

FOOD	Measure or Weight	Food Energy Cal.	Proteins Gms.	Carbo-hydrates Gms.	Fat Gms.	Choles-terol Mg.	Calcium Mg.	Iron Mg.	Sodium Mg.	Vitamin A IU.	Thiamin Mg.	Ribo-flavin Mg.	Niacin C Mg.	Vitamin C Mg.
Apple pie, 2 crust, piecrust made with unenriched flour, sector - 4 in., 1/7 of 9 in. diam. pie (USDA)	1 sector	350	3	51	15	15	11	.4	410	40	.03	.03	.5	1
Apple pie (Hostess)	1 pie	420	3	52	22	15	2%	4%	410	0	15%	6%	8%	4%
Apple pie, frozen (Banquet)	20 oz.	1440	15.9	213.2	58.4		45	1.5	1786	159	.11	.11	1.93	4.5
Apple pie, 24 oz., frozen (Morton)	4 oz.	300	2	43	14	10	0	6%	240	0	6%	4%	4%	6%
Banana cream pie, frozen (Banquet)	14 oz.	1032	8.9	119.6	57.6		544	.5	464	492	.12	.64	.87	4
Banana cream pie, frozen (Morton)	2.66 oz.	200	2	26	10	0	2%	0	115	0	0	4%	0	0
Blueberry pie (Hostess)	1 pie	410	4	52	21	15	2%	4%	410	0	15%	6%	8%	4%
Blueberry pie, frozen (Banquet)	20 oz.	1520	18.7	225.1	60.7		68	3.2	1576	153	.11	.11	1.81	15.3

GRAIN PRODUCTS

FOOD	Measure or Weight	Food Energy Cal.	Proteins Gms.	Carbo-hydrates Gms.	Fat Gms.	Choles-terol Mg.	Calcium Mg.	Iron Mg.	Sodium Mg.	Vitamin A IU.	Thiamin Mg.	Ribo-flavin Mg.	Niacin C Mg.	Vitamin C Mg.
Blueberry pie, 24 oz., frozen (Morton)	4 oz.	300	3	42	14	10	0	6%	250	0	6	4%	4%	4%
Cherry pie, 2 crust (USDA)	1 sector	350	4	52	15	15	19	.4	410	590	.03	.03	.7	Trace
Cherry pie (Hostess)	1 pie	430	4	56	21	15	2%	4%	410	0	15%	6%	8%	4%
Cherry pie, frozen (Banquet)	20 oz.	1366	15.9	203	54.4		57	1.5	1763	2262	.11	Trace	2.61	Trace
Cherry pie, frozen, 24 oz. (Morton)	4 oz.	300	3	42	14	10	0	6%	250	4%	8%	6%	4%	6%
Chocolate cream pie, frozen (Banquet)	14 oz.	1064	11.8	131	54.6		588	.5	381	445	.12	.64	.87	4
Chocolate cream pie, 16 oz., frozen (Morton)	2.66 oz.	220	2	29	12	0	2%	2%	125	0	0	4%	0	0
Custard pie, 1 crust (USDA)	1 sector	285	8	30	14		125	.8	1735	300	.07	.21	.4	0
Custard pie, frozen (Banquet)	20 oz.	1236	28.9	190.5	39.7		454	3.9	1735	1111	.23	.96	1.87	Trace

FOOD	Measure or Weight	Food Energy Cal.	Proteins Gms.	Carbohydrates Gms.	Fat Gms.	Cholesterol Mg.	Calcium Mg.	Iron Mg.	Sodium Mg.	Vitamin A IU.	Thiamin Mg.	Riboflavin Mg.	Niacin C Mg.	Vitamin C Mg.
Lemon pie (Hostess)	1 pie	450	3	56	24	15	2%	2%	410	0	10%	6%	6%	2%
Lemon cream pie, frozen (Banquet)	14 oz.	1008	7.5	131	50.6		580	.8	397	504	.12	.6	.83	6.4
Lemon meringue pie, 1 crust (USDA)	1 sector	305	4	45	12		17	.6		200	.04	.1	.2	4
Mince pie, 2 crust (USDA)	1 sector	365	3	56	16		38	1.4		Trace	.09	.05	.5	1
Mincemeat pie, frozen (Banquet)	20 oz.	1514	18.1	230.8	57.3		170	5.4	2756	57	.34	.23	2.1	6.2
Peach pie (Hostess)	1 pie	450	3	51	21	15	2%	4%	410	0	15%	6%	8%	2%
Peach pie, frozen (Banquet)	20 oz.	1315	17	179.2	59	10	57	3	1644	3992	.11	.23	4.14	11.9
Peach pie, 24 oz., frozen (Morton)	4 oz.	290	2	40	14		0	6%	260	4%	6%	4%	6%	2%
Pumpkin pie, 1 crust (USDA)	1 sector	275	5	32	15		66	.7		3210	.04	.13	.7	Trace
Pumpkin pie mix, plain (Libby's)	1/6 pie	330	8	49	17		15%	10%		130%	8%	25%	2%	6%

GRAIN PRODUCTS

FOOD	Measure or Weight	Food Energy Cal.	Proteins Gms.	Carbo-hydrates Gms.	Fat Gms.	Choles-terol Mg.	Calcium Mg.	Iron Mg.	Sodium Mg.	Vitamin A IU.	Thiamin Mg.	Ribo-flavin Mg.	Niacin C Mg.	Vitamin C Mg.
Pumpkin pie, frozen (Banquet)	20 oz.	1236	21.5	193.9	41.1		272	2.3	1327	12151	.17	.45	2.49	Trace
Pumpkin pie, 24 oz., frozen (Morton)	4 oz.	240	5	35	9	40	8%	4%	300	50%	6%	10%	4%	4%
Piecrust, baked shell made with enriched flour (USDA)	1 shell	900	11	79	60		25	3.1		0	.36	.25	3.2	0
Piecrust mix including stick form, 10 oz. pkg. for double crust (USDA)	1 pkg.	1480	20	141	93		131	1.4		0	.11	.11	2	0
Pie crust mix (Betty Crocker)	1/16 pkg.	120	1	10	8		★	2%		★	4%	2%	2%	★
Piecrust mix, 9 in. single crust (Flako)	1/6 pie	116	1.6	11.7	7		11	.5	147	0	.08	.02	.5	0
Piecrust mix, 2 crust (Pillsbury)	1/6 pie	290	4	27	18		0	6%		0	15%	8%	8%	0

FOOD	Measure or Weight	Food Energy Cal.	Proteins Gms.	Carbo-hydrates Gms.	Fat Gms.	Choles-terol Mg.	Calcium Mg.	Iron Mg.	Sodium Mg.	Vitamin A IU.	Thiamin Mg.	Ribo-flavin Mg.	Niacin C Mg.	Vitamin C Mg.
PIZZA TO PRETZELS														
Pizza, cheese, 5½ in. sector; ⅛ of 14 in. diam. pie (USDA)	1 sector	185	7	27	6		107	.7		290	.04	.12	.7	4
Pizza, cheese (Celeste)	¼ of 20 oz. pizza	321	16.4	35.6	12.6		370	1.7	820	718	.22	.17	1.8	
Pizza, sausage (Celeste)	¼ of 23 oz. pizza	400	17.9	38	19.6		293	3.4	970	450	.39	.18	2.8	
Popcorn, popped, plain, large kernel (USDA)	1 cup	25	1	5	Trace		1	.2		—	—	.01	.1	0
Popcorn, popped with oil and salt (USDA)	1 cup	40	1	5	2		1	.2		—	—	.01	.2	0
Popcorn, popped, sugar coated (USDA)	1 cup	135	2	30	1		2	.5		—	—	.02	.4	0
Popover mix (Flako)	1 large popover	163	7	22.7	4.8		76	1.13	300	268	.15	.2	1.1	
Pop-tarts, cherry (Kellogg's)	1 pastry	210	3	35	6		10%	10%		10%	10%	10%	10%	★

205

GRAIN PRODUCTS

FOOD	Measure or Weight	Food Energy Cal.	Proteins Gms.	Carbo-hydrates Gms.	Fat Gms.	Choles-terol Mg.	Calcium Mg.	Iron Mg.	Sodium Mg.	Vitamin A IU.	Thiamin Mg.	Ribo-flavin Mg.	Niacin Mg.	Vitamin C Mg.
Pop-tarts, frosted, cherry (Kellogg's)	1 pastry	210	3	36	6		10%	10%		10%	10%	10%	10%	★
Pretzels, Dutch, twisted (USDA)	1 pretzel	60	2	12	1		4	.2		0	Trace	Trace	.1	0
Pretzels, thin, twisted (USDA)	1 pretzel	25	1	5	Trace		1	.1		0	Trace	Trace	Trace	0
Pretzels, Veri-thin, Mister Salty (Nabisco)	5 pretzels	100	2	20	1		★	4%		★	4%	2%	4%	★
Pretzel sticks, 3⅛ in. (USDA)	5 sticks	10	Trace	2	Trace		1	Trace		0	Trace	Trace	Trace	0
RICE PRODUCTS														
Rice, brown, long grained, cooked without butter or salt (Uncle Ben's)	⅔ cup	133	2.9	28.5	1.1		6	1.7	6	0	.12	.01	1.8	0
Rice, white, enriched raw (USDA)	1 cup	670	12	149	1		44	5.4[20]		0	.81[20]	.06[20]	6.5[20]	0

FOOD	Measure or Weight	Food Energy Cal.	Proteins Gms.	Carbohydrates Gms.	Fat Gms.	Cholesterol Mg.	Calcium Mg.	Iron Mg.	Sodium Mg.	Vitamin A IU.	Thiamin Mg.	Riboflavin Mg.	Niacin C Mg.	Vitamin C Mg.
Rice, white, cooked (USDA)	1 cup	225	4	50	Trace		21	1.8_{20}		0	$.23_{20}$	$.02_{20}$	2.1_{20}	0
Rice, white, enriched, parboiled (Uncle Ben's)	⅔ cup	121	2.3	27.6	.17		27	.99	3.4	0	.15	.01	1.6	0
Rice, enriched, precooked with butter (Uncle Ben's)	⅔ cup	126	1.9	24.2	2.5		3	.88	37	0	.13	.01	1.1	0
Rice, enriched, precooked, without butter or salt (Uncle Ben's)	⅔ cup	105	1.9	24.1	.09		3	.88	9	0	.13	.01	1	0
Rice, dry mix, chicken flavored, cooked without butter (Uncle Ben's)	½ cup	100	2.6	20.5	.9		24	1.18	416	10	.11	.02	1.4	1.8
Rice mix, fried, prepared with oil (Minute)	½ cup	160	3	25	5		★	6%	630	★	15%	★	8%	★
Rice mix, long grain and wild rice, prepared with butter (Minute)	½ cup	150	3	25	4		★	6%	680	4%	8%	★	6%	2%
Rice mix, Spanish, prepared with butter and tomatoes (Minute)	½ cup	150	3	25	4		★	6%	885	15%	10%	★	8%	25%

GRAIN PRODUCTS

FOOD	Measure or Weight	Food Energy Cal.	Proteins Gms.	Carbo-hydrates Gms.	Fat Gms.	Choles-terol Mg.	Calcium Mg.	Iron Mg.	Sodium Mg.	Vitamin A IU.	Thiamin Mg.	Ribo-flavin Mg.	Niacin C Mg.	Vitamin C Mg.
Rice, frozen, brown rice in beef stock (Green Giant)	1 cup	280	6	48	7		2%	4%		★	2%	6%	6%	10%
Rice, frozen, fiesta, with corn and tomato flavoring (Green Giant)	1 cup	240	4	45	5		2%	10%		20%	20%	4%	10%	25%
Rice, frozen, pilaf, with mushrooms and onions (Green Giant)	1 cup	230	4	45	4		★	8%		★	10%	2%	10%	4%
Rice, frozen, white and wild rice (Green Giant)	1 cup	220	5	43	3		2%	10%		2%	15%	4%	10%	6%
— Cereals														
Cocoa Crispies (Kellogg's)	1 oz.	110	1	26	0		★	10%		25%	25%	25%	25%	25%
Frosted rice cereal (Kellogg's)	1 oz.	110	1	26	0		★	10%		25%	25%	35%	25%	25%
Rice, puffed, added nutrients (USDA)	1 cup	60	1	13	Trace		3	.3		0	.07	.01	.7	0

FOOD	Measure or Weight	Food Energy Cal.	Proteins Gms.	Carbohydrates Gms.	Fat Gms.	Cholesterol Mg.	Calcium Mg.	Iron Mg.	Sodium Mg.	Vitamin A IU.	Thiamin Mg.	Riboflavin Mg.	Niacin C Mg.	Vitamin C Mg.
Rice, puffed (Quaker)	1 cup	56	.9	12.5	.1		3	.26	.3	0	.06	.01	.62	0
Rice Krinkles, frosted (Post)	1 oz.	110	1	26	0		*	4%	225	25%	25%	25%	25%	*
Rice Krispies (Kellogg's)	1 oz.	110	2	25	0		*	10%		25%	25%	25%	25%	25%
ROLLS														
Butter crescent rolls (Pepperidge Farm)	1 roll	130	2	14	6		0	4%	165	2%	6%	4%	4%	0
Cloverleaf or pan rolls, commercial (USDA)	1 roll	85	2	15	2		21	.5		Trace	.08	.05	.6	Trace
Cloverleaf or pan rolls, home recipe (USDA)	1 roll	120	3	20	3		16	.7		30	.09	.09	.8	Trace
Cloverleaf dinner rolls (Pillsbury)	1 roll	100	3	17	2		0	4%	440	0	8%	6%	4%	0
Crescent rolls (Ballard)	2 rolls	190	4	26	8		0	4%	610	0	15%	8%	8%	0
Deli rolls, plain, seeded (Pepperidge Farm)	1 roll	160	6	30	2		4%	8%	240	0	15%	6%	10%	0
Dinner rolls (Pepperidge Farm)	2 rolls	120	3	19	3		2%	4%	200	0	6%	6%	6%	0

GRAIN PRODUCTS

FOOD	Measure or Weight	Food Energy Cal.	Proteins Gms.	Carbo-hydrates Gms.	Fat Gms.	Choles-terol Mg.	Calcium Mg.	Iron Mg.	Sodium Mg.	Vitamin A IU.	Thiamin Mg.	Ribo-flavin Mg.	Niacin C Mg.	Vitamin C Mg.
Dinner rolls (Wonder)	2 oz.	170	4	27	5	0	6%	8%	300	0	15%	8%	10%	0
French rolls, large (Pepperidge Farm)	½ roll	180	6	36	1		2%	8%	445	0	10%	8%	10%	0
Hamburger or frankfurter rolls (USDA)	1 roll	120	3	21	2		30	.8		Trace	.11	.07	.9	Trace
Hamburger (Pepperidge Farm)	1 roll	110	3	19	2		2%	4%	220	0	6%	4%	4%	0
Hamburger or hot dog bun (Wonder)	2 oz.	160	5	29	3	0	6%	8%	310	0	15%	8%	10%	0
Hard, round or rectangular rolls (USDA)	1 roll	155	5	30	2		24	1.2	255	Trace	.13	.12	1.4	Trace
Hot roll mix (Pillsbury)	2 rolls	190	6	31	4		0	6%	255	0	20%	15%	10%	0
Parkerhouse rolls (Pepperidge Farm)	3 rolls	170	5	28	5		4%	6%	250	0	10%	8%	8%	0
Parkerhouse rolls (Pillsbury)	2 rolls	120	3	23	2		0	4%	575	0	10%	6%	6%	0

FOOD	Measure or Weight	Food Energy Cal.	Proteins Gms.	Carbo-hydrates Gms.	Fat Gms.	Choles-terol Mg.	Calcium Mg.	Iron Mg.	Sodium Mg.	Vitamin A IU.	Thiamin Mg.	Riboflavin Mg.	Niacin C Mg.	Vitamin C Mg.
Snowflake rolls (Pillsbury)	2 rolls	140	4	23	4		0	4%	630	0	10%	6%	6%	0
Sweet rolls, cinnamon with icing (Pillsbury)	2 rolls	230	3	34	9		0	6%	505	0	10%	6%	6%	0
SPAGHETTI														
Spaghetti, cooked, tender stage, enriched (USDA)	1 cup	155	5	32	1		11	1.3[19]		0	.20[19]	.11[19]	1.5[19]	0
Spaghetti with meat balls and tomato sauce, home recipe (USDA)	1 cup	330	19	39	12		124	3.7		1590	.25	.3	4	22
Spaghetti 'n beef in tomato sauce, canned (Franco - American)	7½ oz.	250	9	28	11		2%	10%	1105	15%	10%	8%	15%	2%
Spaghetti with meat balls and tomato sauce, canned (USDA)	1 cup	260	12	28	10		53	3.3	945	1000	.15	.18	2.3	5
Spaghetti with meatballs in tomato sauce, canned (Franco - American)	7¼ oz.	230	9	22	11		2%	10%		10%	10%	8%	15%	2%

GRAIN PRODUCTS

FOOD	Measure or Weight	Food Energy Cal.	Proteins Gms.	Carbo-hydrates Gms.	Fat Gms.	Choles-terol Mg.	Calcium Mg.	Iron Mg.	Sodium Mg.	Vitamin A IU.	Thiamin Mg.	Ribo-flavin Mg.	Niacin C Mg.	Vitamin C Mg.
"SpaghettiOs" with little meatballs in tomato sauce, canned (Franco - American)	7½ oz.	230	10	24	10		4%	10%	1125	6%	10%	10%	15%	4%
"SpaghettiOs" with sliced franks in tomato sauce, canned (Franco - American)	7½ oz.	240	9	28	12		4%	10%	990	6%	10%	10%	15%	2%
Spaghetti in tomato sauce with cheese, home recipe (USDA)	1 cup	260	9	37	9		80	2.3		1080	.25	.18	2.3	13
Spaghetti in tomato sauce with cheese, canned (USDA)	1 cup	190	6	38	2		40	2.8		930	.35	.28	4.5	10
Spaghetti in tomato sauce with cheese, canned (Franco - American)	7½ oz.	180	5	34	2		4%	6%	820	15%	15%	8%	15%	★
Spaghetti & meatballs, frozen dinner (Banquet)	11½ oz.	450	14.7	62.9	15.3		82	3.7	1851	3645	.36	.2	3.78	22.5

FOOD	Measure or Weight	Food Energy Cal.	Proteins Gms.	Carbo-hydrates Gms.	Fat Gms.	Choles-terol Mg.	Calcium Mg.	Iron Mg.	Sodium Mg.	Vitamin A IU.	Thiamin Mg.	Ribo-flavin Mg.	Niacin C Mg.	Vitamin C Mg.
Spaghetti and meatballs frozen dinner (Morton)	11 oz.	360	14	59	8	45	6%	20%	1210	10%	15%	15%	20%	30%
Spaghetti and meatballs frozen dinner (Swanson)	12½ oz.	410	14	57	14	28	8%	15%	1150	15%	15%	10%	15%	10%
STUFFING TO WAFFLES														
Stuffing mix, bread, cooked with butter (Uncle Ben's Stuff 'n Such)	½ cup	191	4.3	24.3	8.6		16	40	746	338	.06	.03	.7	1.1
Stuffing mix, bread, cooked without butter (Uncle Ben's Stuff 'n Such)	½ cup	118	4.2	24.2	.6		14	39	647	10	.06	.03	.7	1.1
Stuffing mix, chicken (Stove Top)	½ cup	180	4	20	9		4%	6%	720	6%	10%	6%	6%	★
Stuffing mix, cornbread (Stove Top)	½ cup	170	3	20	8		★	4%	650	6%	6%	4%	4%	★
Stuffing mix, with rice (Stove Top)	½ cup	180	3	23	9		4%	8%	630	6%	10%	4%	8%	★

GRAIN PRODUCTS

FOOD	Measure or Weight	Food Energy Cal.	Proteins Gms.	Carbo-hydrates Gms.	Fat Gms.	Choles-terol Mg.	Calcium Mg.	Iron Mg.	Sodium Mg.	Vitamin A IU.	Thiamin Mg.	Ribo-flavin Mg.	Niacin C Mg.	Vitamin C Mg.
Toast-R-Cakes, blueberry, fresh or frozen (S.B. Thomas)	1 cake	110	2.1	17.4	3.6		25	.7	275		.13	.09	.91	
Toast-R-Cakes, bran, fresh or frozen (S.B. Thomas)	1 cake	115	1.9	19.6	3.2		20	.8	310		.1	.06	.01	
Toast-R-Cakes, corn, fresh or frozen (S.B. Thomas)	1 cake	120	2.2	18.8	3.9		20	.5	325		.09	.06	.68	
Turnover, apple (Pillsbury)	1 turnover	170	2	26	7		0	2%	340	0	6%	4%	4%	0
Turnover, cherry (Pillsbury)	1 turnover	180	2	25	8		0	2%	290	0	4%	2%	2%	6%
Waffles, with enriched flour, 7 in. diam. (USDA)	1 waffle	210	7	28	7		85	1.3		250	.13	.19	1	Trace
Waffles, made with mix, enriched, egg and milk added, 7 in. diam. (USDA)	1 waffle	205	7	27	8		179	1		170	.11	.17	.7	Trace

FOOD	Measure or Weight	Food Energy Cal.	Proteins Gms.	Carbohydrates Gms.	Fat Gms.	Cholesterol Mg.	Calcium Mg.	Iron Mg.	Sodium Mg.	Vitamin A IU.	Thiamin Mg.	Riboflavin Mg.	Niacin C Mg.	Vitamin C Mg.
Waffles, frozen (Aunt Jemima)	2 sections	114	2.3	15.7	4.7		82	.65	320	31	.07	.05	.55	
Waffles, frozen (Eggo)	1 waffle	120	3	17	5		2%	10%		10%	10%	10%	10%	★
Waffles with imitation blueberries, frozen (Eggo)	1 waffle	130	3	17	5		2%	10%		10%	10%	10%	10%	★
WHEAT CEREALS														
Buc Wheats (General Mills)	1 oz.	110	2	23	1		4%	45%		45%	45%	45%	45%	45%
Cream of Wheat, regular (Nabisco)	2½ tbsp.	100	3	22	0		★	45%		★	10%	6%	4%	★
Cream of Wheat, quick	2½ tbsp.	100	3	21	0		★	45%		★	10%	6%	4%	★
Farina, quick-cooking, enriched, cooked (USDA)	1 cup	105	3	22	Trace	0	147	.7[19]		0	.12[19]	.07[19]	1[19]	0
Farina, enriched (H-O Cream)	2 tbsp.	80	3	17	0	0	★	4%	<5	★	6%	2%	4%	★
Farina, enriched, uncooked (Quaker)	1/6 cup	100	2.5	22.1	.2		5	.8	.6		.12	.07	1	

GRAIN PRODUCTS

FOOD	Measure or Weight	Food Energy Cal.	Proteins Gms.	Carbohydrates Gms.	Fat Gms.	Cholesterol Mg.	Calcium Mg.	Iron Mg.	Sodium Mg.	Vitamin A IU.	Thiamin Mg.	Riboflavin Mg.	Niacin C Mg.	Vitamin C Mg.
Grape-nuts flakes (Post)	1 oz.	100	2	23	1		★	10%	200	25%	25%	25%	25%	★
Shredded wheat biscuit	1 biscuit	80	2	17	1		★	4%		★	2%	★	6%	★
Spoon size shredded wheat (Nabisco)	⅔ cup	110	3	23	1		★	6%		★	4%	★	8%	★
Sugar Smacks (Kellogg's)	1 oz.	110	2	25	0		★	10%		25%	25%	25%	25%	25%
Wheat, puffed, added nutrients (USDA)	1 cup	55	2	12	Trace		4	.6		0	.08	.03	1.2	0
Wheat, puffed (Quaker)	1 cup	51	1.9	11.2	.2		3	.6	.3	0	.08	.03	1.1	
Wheat, shredded, plain (USDA)	1 biscuit	90	2	20	1		11	.9		0	.06	.03	1.1	0
Wheat, shredded (Quaker)	2 biscuits	135	3.6	28.7	.7		15	1	2	0	.08	.03	1.5	
Wheat flakes, added nutrients (USDA)	1 cup	105	3	24	Trace		12	1.3		0	.19	.04	1.5	0
Wheat flakes, Pep (Kellogg's)	1 oz.	100	2	24	0		★	10%		25%	25%	25%	25%	25%

FOOD	Measure or Weight	Food Energy Cal.	Proteins Gms.	Carbo-hydrates Gms.	Fat Gms.	Choles-terol Mg.	Calcium Mg.	Iron Mg.	Sodium Mg.	Vitamin A IU.	Thiamin Mg.	Ribo-flavin Mg.	Niacin C Mg.	Vitamin C Mg.
Wheaties, whole wheat cereal (General Mills)	1 oz.	110	2	23	1		*	25%		25%	25%	25%	25%	25%

FATS, OILS, SALAD DRESSINGS

FATS, OILS, SALAD DRESSINGS

FOOD	Measure or Weight	Food Energy Cal.	Proteins Gms.	Carbo- hydrates Gms.	Fat Gms.	Choles- terol Mg.	Calcium Mg.	Iron Mg.	Sodium Mg.	Vitamin A IU.	Thiamin Mg.	Ribo- flavin Mg.	Niacin C Mg.	Vitamin C Mg.
FATS														
Butter, pat, 1 in. sq. 1/3 in. high (USDA)	1 pat	35	Trace	Trace	4		1	0		170[21]	—	—	—	0
Butter, lightly salted (Breakstone Sugar Creek Foods)	1 pat	100	.4	.5	80%	29								
Butter, regular (USDA)	1 tbsp.	100	Trace	Trace	12		3	0		470[21]	—	—	—	0
Butter, sweet unsalted (Breakstone Sugar Creek Foods)	1 pat	100	.5	.6	80%	29								
Butter, whipped (USDA)	1 tbsp.	65	Trace	Trace	8		2	0		310[21]	—	—	—	0
Butter, whipped, pat 1 1/4 in. sq. 1/3 in. high (USDA)	1 pat	25	Trace	Trace	3		1	0		130[21]	—	—	—	0
Butter, whipped, lightly salted (Breakstone Sugar Creek Foods)	1 pat	65	.4	.5	80%	19								

FOOD	Measure or Weight	Food Energy Cal.	Proteins Gms.	Carbohydrates Gms.	Fat Gms.	Cholesterol Mg.	Calcium Mg.	Iron Mg.	Sodium Mg.	Vitamin A IU.	Thiamin Mg.	Riboflavin Mg.	Niacin C Mg.	Vitamin C Mg.
Butter, whipped sweet (Breakstone Sugar Creek Foods)	1 pat	65	.5	.6	80%	19								
Lard (USDA)	1 tbsp.	115	0	0	13		0	0		0	0	0	0	0
Margarine, regular (USDA)	1 tbsp.	100	Trace	Trace	12		3	0		470_{22}	—	—	—	0
Margarine (Blue Bonnet)	1 tbsp.	100	.07	.1	11.2				110					
Margarine (Fleischmann's)	1 tbsp.	100	.07	.1	11.2				110					
Margarine (Mazola)	1 tbsp.	100	0	0	11	0	★	★	115	10%	★	★	★	★
Margarine (Nucoa)	1 tbsp.	100	0	0	11	0	★	★	160	★	★	★	★	★
Margarine, soft (USDA)	1 tbsp.	100	Trace	Trace	11		3	0		470_{22}	—	—	—	0
Margarine, soft (Blue Bonnet)	1 tbsp.	100	.07	.1	11.2				110					
Margarine, soft (Fleischmann's)	1 tbsp.	100	.07	.1	11.2				110					
Margarine, soft (Nucoa)	1 tbsp.	90	0	0	10	0	★	★	145	10%	★	★	★	★

FATS, OILS, SALAD DRESSING

FOOD	Measure or Weight	Food Energy Cal.	Proteins Gms.	Carbo-hydrates Gms.	Fat Gms.	Choles-terol Mg.	Calcium Mg.	Iron Mg.	Sodium Mg.	Vitamin A IU.	Thiamin Mg.	Ribo-flavin Mg.	Niacin C Mg.	Vitamin C Mg.
Margarine, unsalted (Fleischmann's)	1 tbsp.	100	.07	.1	11.2				1.4					
Margarine, unsalted (Mazola)	1 tbsp.	100	0	0	11	0	★	★	<1	10%	★	★	★	★
Margarine, whipped (Blue Bonnet)	1 tbsp.	70	.04	.06	7.4				70					
Vegetable fats (USDA)	1 tbsp.	110	0	0	13	0	0	0		—	0	0	0	0
Crisco (Proctor & Gamble)	1 tbsp.	110	0	0	12	0	★	★	0	★	★	★	★	★
Fluffo (Proctor & Gamble)	1 tbsp.	110	0	0	12	0	★	★	0	★	★	★	★	★
OILS														
Corn oil (USDA)	1 tbsp.	125	0	0	14	0	0	0	0	—	0	0	0	0
Corn oil (Mazola)	1 tbsp.	120	0	0	14	0	★	★	0	★	★	★	★	★
Cottonseed oil (USDA)	1 tbsp.	125	0	0	14	0	0	0	0	—	0	0	0	0

FOOD	Measure or Weight	Food Energy Cal.	Proteins Gms.	Carbohydrates Gms.	Fat Gms.	Cholesterol Mg.	Calcium Mg.	Iron Mg.	Sodium Mg.	Vitamin A IU.	Thiamin Mg.	Riboflavin Mg.	Niacin C Mg.	Vitamin C Mg.
Crisco oil (Proctor & Gamble)	1 tbsp.	120	0	0	14	0	★	★	0	★	★	★	★	★
Olive oil (USDA)	1 tbsp.	125	0	0	14		0	0		—	0	0	0	0
Peanut oil (USDA)	1 tbsp.	125	0	0	14		0	0		—	0	0	0	0
Safflower oil (USDA)	1 tbsp.	125	0	0	14		0	0		—	0	0	0	0
Soybean oil (USDA)	1 tbsp.	125	0	0	14		0	0		—	0	0	0	0
Soybean and cottonseed oil (Wesson)	1 tbsp.	120	0	0	14	0	★	★		★	★	★	★	★
SALAD DRESSINGS														
Blue cheese dressing (USDA)	1 tbsp.	75	1	1	8		12	Trace		30	Trace	.02	Trace	Trace
Blue cheese chunky (Wish - Bone)	1 tbsp.	70	0	1	8	0	★	★		★	★	2	★	★
Caesar dressing (Wish - Bone)	1 tbsp.	80	0	1	8	0	★	★		★	★	★	★	★
Commercial, mayonnaise type dressing (USDA)	1 tbsp.	65	Trace	2	6		2	Trace		30	Trace	Trace	Trace	—

FATS, OILS, SALAD DRESSING

FOOD	Measure or Weight	Food Energy Cal.	Proteins Gms.	Carbo-hydrates Gms.	Fat Gms.	Choles-terol Mg.	Calcium Mg.	Iron Mg.	Sodium Mg.	Vitamin A IU.	Thiamin Mg.	Ribo-flavin Mg.	Niacin C Mg.	Vitamin C Mg.
Commercial, mayonnaise, special dietary, low calorie (USDA)	1 tbsp.	20	Trace	1	2		3	Trace		40	Trace	Trace	Trace	—
Diet Mayo 7, imitation mayonnaise (Bennett's)	1 tbsp.	25	0	2	2				165					—
French dressing, regular (USDA)	1 tbsp.	65	Trace	3	6		2	.1		—	—	—	—	—
French dressing (Bennett's)	1 tbsp.	55	0	2	5				220					
French dressing, deluxe (Wish - Bone)	1 tbsp.	60	0	2	5	0	★	★		★	★	★	★	★
French dressing, garlic (Wish - Bone)	1 tbsp.	70	0	3	6	0	★	★		★	★	★	★	★
French dressing, special dietary, low-fat with artificial sweeteners (USDA)	1 tbsp.	Trace	Trace	Trace	Trace		2	.1		—	—	—	—	—

224

FOOD	Measure or Weight	Food Energy Cal.	Proteins Gms.	Carbohydrates Gms.	Fat Gms.	Cholesterol Mg.	Calcium Mg.	Iron Mg.	Sodium Mg.	Vitamin A IU.	Thiamin Mg.	Riboflavin Mg.	Niacin C Mg.	Vitamin C Mg.
Home cooked dressing, boiled (USDA)	1 tbsp.	25	1	2	2		14	.1		80	.01	.03	Trace	Trace
Italian dressing (Wish - Bone)	1 tbsp.	80	0	1	8	0	★	★		★	★	★	★	★
Low calorie French style dressing (Diet)	1 tbsp.	25	0	3	1				150					
Low calorie Italian dressing (Diet)	1 tbsp.	7	0	1	.4				290					
Low calorie Italian salad dressing (Good Seasons)	1 tbsp.	8	0	2	0		★	★	160	★	★	★	★	★
Low calorie Italian salad dressing (Wish - Bone)	1 tbsp.	18	0	1	2	0	★	★		★	★	★	★	★
Low calorie Russian dressing (Wish - Bone)	1 tbsp.	25	0	5	1	0	★	★		★	★	★	★	★
Low calorie Thousand Island dressing (Wish - Bone)	1 tbsp.	70	0	3	7	5	★	★		★	★	★	★	★
Mayonnaise (USDA)	1 tbsp.	100	Trace	Trace	11		3	.1		40	Trace	.01	Trace	—

FATS, OILS, SALAD DRESSING

FOOD	Measure or Weight	Food Energy Cal.	Proteins Gms.	Carbohydrates Gms.	Fat Gms.	Cholesterol Mg.	Calcium Mg.	Iron Mg.	Sodium Mg.	Vitamin A IU.	Thiamin Mg.	Riboflavin Mg.	Niacin C Mg.	Vitamin C Mg.
Mayonnaise (Bennett's)	1 tbsp.	110	0	0	12				75					
Real Mayonnaise (Hellmann's/Best Foods)	1 tbsp.	100	0	0	11	10	★	★	80	★	★	★	★	★
Russian dressing (Wish - Bone)	1 tbsp.	60	0	7	3	0	★	★		★	★	★	★	★
Salad dressing (Bennett's)	1 tbsp.	50	0	2	6				125					
Spin Blend salad dressing (Hellmann's)	1 tbsp.	60	0	3	5	10	★	★	105	★	★	★	★	★
Thousand Island dressing (USDA)	1 tbsp.	80	Trace	3	8		2	.1		50	Trace	Trace	Trace	Trace
Thousand Island dressing (Wish - Bone)	1 tbsp.	70	0	3	7	5	★	★		★	★	★	★	★

SWEETS, SUGARS, SYRUPS

SWEETS, SUGARS, SYRUPS

SWEETS — Cake Icings

FOOD	Measure or Weight	Food Energy Cal.	Proteins Gms.	Carbo-hydrates Gms.	Fat Gms.	Choles-terol Mg.	Calcium Mg.	Iron Mg.	Sodium Mg.	Vitamin A IU.	Thiamin Mg.	Ribo-flavin Mg.	Niacin C Mg.	Vitamin C Mg.
Boiled icing, coconut (USDA)	1 cup	605	3	124	13		10	.8		0	.02	.07	.3	0
Boiled white icing, (USDA)	1 cup	300	1	76	0		2	Trace		0	Trace	.03	Trace	0
Chocolate icing made with milk and table fat (USDA)	1 cup	1035	9	185	38		165	3.3		580	.06	.28	.6	1
Chocolate fudge, icing mix (Pillsbury)	for 1/12 cake	170	<1	28	6		★	★	75	★	★	★	★	★
Chocolate, ready to spread (Betty Crocker)	1/12 can	170	0	25	8		★	2%		★	★	2%	★	★
Chocolate fudge, ready to spread (Pillsbury)	for 1/12 cake	160	<1	24	7		★	★	90	★	★	★	★	★
Creamy fudge from mix with water only (USDA)	1 cup	830	7	183	16		96	2.7		Trace	.05	.2	.7	Trace
Creamy chocolate fudge, (Betty Crocker)	1/12 pkg.	160	0	32	3		★	2%		★	★	2%	★	★

228

FOOD	Measure or Weight	Food Energy Cal.	Proteins Gms.	Carbohydrates Gms.	Fat Gms.	Cholesterol Mg.	Calcium Mg.	Iron Mg.	Sodium Mg.	Vitamin A IU.	Thiamin Mg.	Riboflavin Mg.	Niacin C Mg.	Vitamin C Mg.
Creamy, orange (Betty Crocker)	1/12 pkg.	150	0	30	3		★	★		★	★	★	★	★
Creamy, white (Betty Crocker)	1/12 pkg.	160	0	33	3		★	★		★	★	★	★	★
Fluffy chocolate (Betty Crocker)	1/12 pkg.	80	0	13	3		★	★		★	★	0	★	★
Fluffy white (Betty Crocker)	1/12 pkg.	60	0	16	0		★	★		★	★	0	★	★
Fluffy white (Pillsbury)	for 1/12 cake	70	0	17	0		6%	0	85	0	0	0	0	0
Lemon icing mix (Pillsbury)	for 1/12 cake	160	0	29	5		★	★	15	★	★	★	★	★
Lemon ready to spread (Pillsbury)	for 1/12 cake	160	0	27	6		★	★	45	★	★	★	★	★
Orange ready to spread (Betty Crocker)	1/12 can	160	0	26	6		★	0		★	★	0	★	★

SWEETS, SUGARS, SYRUPS

— Candy

FOOD	Measure or Weight	Food Energy Cal.	Proteins Gms.	Carbo-hydrates Gms.	Fat Gms.	Choles-terol Mg.	Calcium Mg.	Iron Mg.	Sodium Mg.	Vitamin A IU.	Thiamin Mg.	Ribo-flavin Mg.	Niacin C Mg.	Vitamin C Mg.
Caramels, plain or chocolate (USDA)	1 oz.	115	1	22	3		42	.4		Trace	.01	.05	.1	Trace
Chocolate, milk, plain (USDA)	1 oz.	145	2	16	9		65	.3		80	.02	.1	.1	Trace
Chocolate, milk (Hershey)	1.05 oz.	160	2	17	10	10	6%	2%	25	★	★	4%	★	★
Chocolate, milk, with almonds (Hershey)	1.05 oz.	160	3	15	10	5	6%	2%	20	★	★	4%	★	★
Chocolate coated peanuts (USDA)	1 oz.	160	5	11	12		33	.4		Trace	.1	.05	2.1	Trace
Fondant, mints, uncoated, candy corn (USDA)	1 oz.	105	Trace	25	1		4	.3		0	Trace	Trace	Trace	0
Fudge, plain (USDA)	1 oz.	115	1	21	4		22	.3		Trace	.01	.03	.1	Trace
Gum drops (USDA)	1 oz.	100	Trace	25	Trace		2	.1		0	0	Trace	Trace	0
Hard Candy (USDA)	1 oz.	110	0	28	Trace		6	.5		0	0	0	0	0

FOOD	Measure or Weight	Food Energy Cal.	Proteins Gms.	Carbo-hydrates Gms.	Fat Gms.	Choles-terol Mg.	Calcium Mg.	Iron Mg.	Sodium Mg.	Vitamin A IU.	Thiamin Mg.	Ribo-flavin Mg.	Niacin Mg.	Vitamin C Mg.
Kisses (Hershey)	1 oz. or 6 pieces	150	2	15	9		4%	★	20	★	★	4%	★	★
Marshmallows (USDA)	1 oz.	90	1	23	Trace		5	.5		0	0	Trace	Trace	0
Mr. Goodbar (Hershey)	1.3 oz.	210	5	18	13	5	4%	2%	15	★	2%	4%	8%	0
Peanut butter cups (Reese)	1.2 oz.	190	4	18	11	5	2%	2%	100	★	★	2%	8%	★
— Chocolate Flavorings														
Chocolate flavored beverage powder, with nonfat dried milk (USDA)	1 oz.	100	5	20	1		167	.5		10	.04	.21	.2	1
Chocolate flavored beverage powder without nonfat dried milk (USDA)	1 oz.	100	1	25	1		9	.6		—	.01	.03	.1	0
Chocolate flavored syrup, fudge type (USDA)	1 fl. oz.	125	2	20	5		48	.5		60	.02	.08	.2	Trace
Chocolate flavored syrup or topping, thin type (USDA)	1 fl. oz.	90	1	24	1		6	.6		Trace	.01	.03	.2	0

SWEETS, SUGARS, SYRUPS

FOOD	Measure or Weight	Food Energy Cal.	Proteins Gms.	Carbo-hydrates Gms.	Fat Gms.	Choles-terol Mg.	Calcium Mg.	Iron Mg.	Sodium Mg.	Vitamin A IU.	Thiamin Mg.	Ribo-flavin Mg.	Niacin Mg.	Vitamin C Mg.
Chocolate flavored syrup (Bosco)	1 tbsp.	50	0	13	0		★	25%	35	15%	★	6%	10%	★
Chocolate flavored syrup (Hershey)	1 oz., 2 tbsp.	90	1	22	1		★	★	15	★	★	★	★	★
Cocoa (Hershey)	1 oz.	120	6	14	4	0	4%	10%	5	★	★	4%	★	★
Hot cocoa mix (Hershey)	1 oz.	110	3	20	2	0	8%	2%	120	★	2%	6%	★	★
— Honey														
Honey, strained or extracted (USDA)	1 tbsp.	65	Trace	17	0		1	.1		0	Trace	.01	.1	Trace
— Jams, Jellies and Preserves														
Jams and preserves (USDA)	1 tbsp.	55	Trace	14	Trace		4	.2		Trace	Trace	.01	Trace	Trace
Jellies (USDA)	1 tbsp.	50	Trace	13	Trace		4	.3		Trace	Trace	.01	Trace	1
Apple jelly (S & W Nutradiet)	1 tsp.	3	0	1	0		0	0		0	0	0	0	0

FOOD	Measure or Weight	Food Energy Cal.	Proteins Gms.	Carbohydrates Gms.	Fat Gms.	Cholesterol Mg.	Calcium Mg.	Iron Mg.	Sodium Mg.	Vitamin A IU.	Thiamin Mg.	Riboflavin Mg.	Niacin Mg.	Vitamin C Mg.
Concord grape jelly (S & W Nutradiet)	1 tsp.	3	0	1	0		0	0		0	0	0	0	0
Raspberry jam (S & W Nutradiet)	1 tsp.	4	0	1	0		0	0		0	0	0	0	0
Strawberry jam (S & W Nutradiet)	1 tsp.	4	0	1	0		0	0		0	0	0	0	0
— Molasses —														
Molasses, cane, light (USDA)	1 tbsp.	50	—	13	—		33	.9		—	.01	.01	Trace	—
Molasses, blackstrap (USDA)	1 tbsp.	45	—	11	—		137	3.2		—	.02	.04	.4	—
SUGARS														
Sugar, brown, firm packed (USDA)	1 cup	820	0	212	0		187	7.5		0	.02	.07	.4	0
Sugar, powdered, stirred before measuring (USDA)	1 cup	460	0	119	0		0	.1		0	0	0	0	0
Sugar, white, granulated (USDA)	1 cup	770	0	199	0		0	.2		0	0	0	0	0

SWEETS, SUGARS, SYRUPS

FOOD	Measure or Weight	Food Energy Cal.	Proteins Gms.	Carbo-hydrates Gms.	Fat Gms.	Choles-terol Mg.	Calcium Mg.	Iron Mg.	Sodium Mg.	Vitamin A IU.	Thiamin Mg.	Ribo-flavin Mg.	Niacin C Mg.	Vitamin C Mg.
Sugar, white granulated (USDA)	1 tbsp.	40	0	11	0		0	Trace		0	0	0	0	0
SYRUPS														
Imitation maple syrup (Karo)	1 tbsp.	60	0	15	0		★	★	20	★	★	★	★	★
Light corn syrup (Karo)	1 tbsp.	60	0	15	0		★	★	25	★	★	★	★	★
Pancake syrup (Golden Griddle)	1 tbsp.	50	0	13	0		★	★	1	★	★	★	★	★
Pancake and waffle syrup (Karo)	1 tbsp.	60	0	15	0		★	★	20	★	★	★	★	★
Pancake syrup (S & W Nutradiet)	1 tsp.	4	0	1	0		0	0		0	0	0	0	0
Syrup, sorghum (USDA)	1 tbsp.	55	—	14	—		35	2.6		—	—	.02	Trace	—
Syrup, table blend (USDA)	1 tbsp.	60	0	14	0		9	.8		0	0	0	0	0
Syrup (Aunt Jemima)	¼ cup	212	0	54	0		5	.2	2	0	0	0	0	0

MISCELLANEOUS ITEMS

MISCELLANEOUS ITEMS

FOOD	Measure or Weight	Food Energy Cal.	Proteins Gms.	Carbo- hydrates Gms.	Fat Gms.	Choles- terol Mg.	Calcium Mg.	Iron Mg.	Sodium Mg.	Vitamin A IU.	Thiamin Mg.	Ribo- flavin Mg.	Niacin Mg.	Vitamin C Mg.
BEVERAGES — Alcoholic														
Beer (USDA)	12 fl. oz.	150	1	14	0		18	Trace		—	.01	.11	2.2	—
86 proof gin, rum, vodka, whiskey (USDA)	1½ fl. oz.	105	—	Trace	—		—	—		—	—	—	—	—
90 proof gin, rum, vodka, whiskey (USDA)	1½ fl. oz.	110	—	Trace	—		—	—		—	—	—	—	—
100 proof gin, rum, vodka, whiskey (USDA)	1½ fl. oz.	125	—	Trace	—		—	—		—	—	—	—	—
Wine, dessert (USDA)	3½ fl. oz.	140	Trace	8	0		8	—		—	.01	.02	.2	—
Wine, table (USDA)	3½ fl. oz.	85	Trace	4	0		9	.4		—	Trace	.01	.1	—
— Carbonated, Sweetened														
Carbonated water (USDA)	12 fl. oz.	115	0	29	0		—	—		0	0	0	0	0
Cola type (USDA)	12 fl. oz.	145	0	37	0		—	—		0	0	0	0	0

FOOD	Measure or Weight	Food Energy Cal.	Proteins Gms.	Carbo-hydrates Gms.	Fat Gms.	Choles-terol Mg.	Calcium Mg.	Iron Mg.	Sodium Mg.	Vitamin A IU.	Thiamin Mg.	Ribo-flavin Mg.	Niacin C Mg.	Vitamin C Mg.
Ginger Ale (USDA)	12 fl. oz.	115	0	29	0		—	—		0	0	0	0	0
Root beer (USDA)	12 fl. oz.	150	0	39	0		—	—		0	0	0	0	0
BREAKFAST FOODS														
Breakfast links (Morningstar)	3 links	180	11	7	12	0	★	8%	680	★	20%	10%	30%	★
Breakfast patties (Morningstar)	2 patties	200	12	8	13	0	★	8%	875	★	25%	10%	35%	★
Breakfast slices (Morningstar)	2 slices	130	10	6	7	0	★	8%	900	★	30%	10%	25%	★
Breakfast strips (Morningstar)	4 strips	100	5	3	7	0	★	4%	550	★	10%	6%	8%	★
CHOCOLATE, BAKING														
Chocolate, bitter or baking (USDA)	1 oz.	145	3	8	15		22	1.9		20	.01	.07	.4	0
Chocolate, baking (Hershey)	1 oz.	190	3	7	16	0	2%	10%	5	★	★	4%	2%	★
Chocolate, semi-sweet, small pieces (USDA)	1 cup	860	7	97	61		51	4.4		30	.02	.14	.9	0

MISCELLANEOUS ITEMS

FOOD	Measure or Weight	Food Energy Cal.	Proteins Gms.	Carbo-hydrates Gms.	Fat Gms.	Choles-terol Mg.	Calcium Mg.	Iron Mg.	Sodium Mg.	Vitamin A IU.	Thiamin Mg.	Ribo-flavin Mg.	Niacin C Mg.	Vitamin C Mg.
Chocolate flavored baking chips, dark (Hershey)	¼ cup	210	2	23	12		★	★	100	★	★	★	★	★
GELATIN														
Gelatin, plain, dry powder in envelope (USDA)	1 envelope	25	6	0	Trace		—	—		—	—	—	—	—
Gelatin, unflavored (Knox)	1 envelope	25	6	0	0		★	★		★	★	★	★	★
Gelatin dessert powder package (USDA)	3 oz. package	315	8	75	0		—	—		—	—	—	—	—
Gelatin dessert prepared with water (USDA)	1 cup	140	4	34	0		—	—		—	—	—	—	—
Gelatin, dessert, cherry (Jello)	½ cup	80	2	18	0		★	★	75	★	★	★	★	★
Gelatin dessert, low calorie (D-Zerta)	½ cup	8	2	0	0		★	★	8	★	★	★	★	★

238

FOOD	Measure or Weight	Food Energy Cal.	Proteins Gms.	Carbohydrates Gms.	Fat Gms.	Cholesterol Mg.	Calcium Mg.	Iron Mg.	Sodium Mg.	Vitamin A IU.	Thiamin Mg.	Riboflavin Mg.	Niacin C Mg.	Vitamin C Mg.
Gelatin dessert, strawberry (Jello)	½ cup	80	2	19	0		★	★	40	★	★	★	★	★
Gelatin desserts (Royal)	½ cup	80	2	18.9	0				90					
GRAVY														
Gravy, canned, beef (Franco - American)	2 oz.	35	2	3	2		★	2%	290	0	★	★	★	0
Gravy, canned, chicken (Franco - American)	2 oz.	55	1	3	4		★	★	285	2%	★	★	★	0
Gravy mix, brown (Pillsbury)	¼ cup	15	0	3	0		★	★	270	★	★	★	★	★
Gravy mix, chicken (Pillsbury)	¼ cup	30	<1	4	1		★	★	200	★	★	★	★	★
OLIVES AND PICKLES														
Olives, green (USDA)	4 medium, 3 extra large, or 2 giant	15	Trace	Trace	2		8	.2		40	—	—	—	—	—

MISCELLANEOUS ITEMS

FOOD	Measure or Weight	Food Energy Cal.	Proteins Gms.	Carbo-hydrates Gms.	Fat Gms.	Choles-terol Mg.	Calcium Mg.	Iron Mg.	Sodium Mg.	Vitamin A IU.	Thiamin Mg.	Ribo-flavin Mg.	Niacin C Mg.	Vitamin C Mg.
Olives, ripe, mission (USDA)	2 large or 3 small	15	Trace	Trace	2		9	.1		10	Trace	Trace	—	—
Pickles, bread and butter (Fanning's)	100 gms.	45	.6	11.5	.1		25	1.2	525	160		Trace		
Pickles, dill, medium, whole 3¾ in. long, 1¼ in. diam. (USDA)	1 pickle	10	1	1	Trace		17	.7		70	Trace	.01	Trace	4
Pickles, fresh, sliced, 1½ in. diam., ¼ in thick (USDA)	2 slices	10	Trace	3	Trace		5	.3		20	Trace	Trace	Trace	1
Pickles, gherkin, sweet, small, whole approx. 2½ in. long, ¾ in. diam. (USDA)	1 pickle	20	Trace	6	Trace		2	.2		10	Trace	Trace	Trace	1
Pickle relish, finely chopped, sweet (USDA)	1 tbsp.	20	Trace	5	Trace		3	.1		—	—	—	—	—

PUDDINGS

FOOD	Measure or Weight	Food Energy Cal.	Proteins Gms.	Carbo-hydrates Gms.	Fat Gms.	Choles-terol Mg.	Calcium Mg.	Iron Mg.	Sodium Mg.	Vitamin A IU.	Thiamin Mg.	Ribo-flavin Mg.	Niacin Mg.	Vitamin C Mg.
Chocolate pudding, home recipe with starch base (USDA)	1 cup	385	8	67	12		250	1.3		390	.05	.36	.3	1
Chocolate pudding, regular (Royal)	½ cup	190	5.1	31.7	5.4				140					
Chocolate pudding and pie filling (Jello)	½ cup	170	5	28	5		15%	2%	205	4%	2%	15%	★	2%
Chocolate pudding, instant (Royal)	½ cup	190	5	31.8	5.2				320					
Chocolate pudding and pie filling, instant (Jello)	½ cup	190	5	34	5		15%	★	515	4%	2%	10%	★	★
Chocolate pudding cup (Del Monte)	5 oz.	190	4	31	6		10%	6%	330	★	2%	10%	2%	★
Chocolate snack pack pudding (Hunt)	5 oz.	180	3	24	10		4%	6%		★	★	8%	★	★
Lemon pie filling (Royal)	1 sector	220	2.8	39.8	5.9		★		260					
Lemon pudding and pie filling (Jello)	1/6 of 9 in. pie	180	2	38	2		★	2%	115	4%	★	2%	★	★

MISCELLANEOUS ITEMS

FOOD	Measure or Weight	Food Energy Cal.	Proteins Gms.	Carbohydrates Gms.	Fat Gms.	Cholesterol Mg.	Calcium Mg.	Iron Mg.	Sodium Mg.	Vitamin A IU.	Thiamin Mg.	Riboflavin Mg.	Niacin C Mg.	Vitamin C Mg.
Lemon pudding and pie filling, instant (Jello)	½ cup	180	4	31	5		15%	★	425	4%	2%	10%	★	★
Pudding mix, dry form, 4 oz. pkg. (USDA)	1 pkg.	410	3	103	2		23	1.8		Trace	.02	.08	.5	0
Tapioca, dry, quick cooking	1 cup	535	1	131	Trace		15	.6		0	0	0	0	0
Tapioca dessert, apple (USDA)	1 cup	295	1	74	Trace		8	.5		30	Trace	Trace	Trace	Trace
Tapioca pudding, chocolate (Jello)	½ cup	170	5	28	5		15%	★	210	4%	2%	10%	★	2%
Tapioca pudding, vanilla (Jello)	½ cup	170	4	28	5		15%	★	170	4%	2%	10%	★	2%
Tapioca snack pack pudding (Hunt)	5 oz.	130	3	23	5		8%	★		★	10%	15%	★	★
Vanilla pudding, home recipe with starch base (USDA)	1 cup	285	9	41	10		298	Trace		410	.08	.41	.3	2

FOOD	Measure or Weight	Food Energy Cal.	Proteins Gms.	Carbohydrates Gms.	Fat Gms.	Cholesterol Mg.	Calcium Mg.	Iron Mg.	Sodium Mg.	Vitamin A IU.	Thiamin Mg.	Riboflavin Mg.	Niacin C Mg.	Vitamin C Mg.
Vanilla pudding, regular (Royal)	½ cup	160	4.3	26.4	4.5				230					
Vanilla pudding and pie filling (Jello)	½ cup	170	4	27	5		15%	★	250	4%	2%	10%	★	2%
Vanilla pudding, instant (Royal)	½ cup	190	4.3	28.8	4.8				310					
Vanilla pudding and pie filling, instant (Jello)	½ cup	180	4	31	5		15%	★	435	4%	2%	10%	★	★
Vanilla pudding cup (Del Monte)	5 oz.	190	3	32	5		10%	★	320	★	2%	10%	2%	★
Vanilla snack pack pudding (Hunt)	5 oz.	190	2	26	10		6%	★		★	★	10%	★	★
Vanilla pudding and pie filling, low calorie (D - Zerta)	½ cup	70	5	13	0		15%	★	140	★	4%	15%	★	★
SOUPS — Canned, Condensed														
Bean with pork with equal volume of water (USDA)	1 cup	170	8	22	6		63	2.3		650	.13	.08	1	3

MISCELLANEOUS ITEMS

FOOD	Measure or Weight	Food Energy Cal.	Proteins Gms.	Carbo-hydrates Gms.	Fat Gms.	Choles-terol Mg.	Calcium Mg.	Iron Mg.	Sodium Mg.	Vitamin A IU.	Thiamin Mg.	Ribo-flavin Mg.	Niacin C Mg.	Vitamin C Mg.
Beef broth, bouillon consomme with equal vol. of water (USDA)	1 cup	30	5	3	5		Trace	.5		Trace	Trace	.02	1.2	—
Beef broth, bouillon (Campbell)	10 oz.	35	4	3	1		★	★	1055	0	★	★	2%	2%
Beef Noodle (USDA)	1 cup	70	4	7	3		7	1		50	.05	.07	1	Trace
Beef Noodle (Campbell)	10 oz.	90	5	10	3		★	4%	1055	6%	4%	4%	8%	0
Clam chowder, Manhattan type with tomatoes, without milk (USDA)	1 cup	80	2	12	3		34	1		880	.02	.02	1	—
Clam chowder, Manhattan style (Campbell)	10 oz.	100	2	15	3		2%	6%	1030	15%	2%	2%	4%	6%
Clam chowder, Manhattan (Doxsee)	8 oz.	100	4	18	3				930					
Clam chowder, New England (Campbell)	10 oz.	100	6	13	3		2%	6%	1075	★	★	2%	4%	4%

FOOD	Measure or Weight	Food Energy Cal.	Proteins Gms.	Carbo- hydrates Gms.	Fat Gms.	Choles- terol Mg.	Calcium Mg.	Iron Mg.	Sodium Mg.	Vitamin A IU.	Thiamin Mg.	Ribo- flavin Mg.	Niacin Mg.	Vitamin C Mg.
Clam chowder, New England with milk (Doxsee)	8 oz.	190	10	27	7				980					
Cream of chicken (USDA)	1 cup	95	3	8	6		24	.5		410	.02	.05	.5	Trace
Cream of chicken with equal volume of milk (USDA)	1 cup	180	7	15	10		172	.5		610	.05	.27	.7	2
Cream of chicken (Campbell)	10 oz.	140	4	10	9		2%	2%	1225	10%	2%	2%	4%	0
Cream of mushroom (USDA)	1 cup	135	2	10	10		41	.5		70	.02	.12	.7	Trace
Cream of mushroom with equal volume of milk (USDA)	1 cup	215	7	16	14		191	.5		250	.05	.34	.7	1
Cream of mushroom (Campbell)	10 oz.	150	2	11	11		2%	2%	990	0	2%	6%	4%	0
Cream of Tomato with equal volume of milk (USDA)	1 cup	175	7	23	7		168	.8		1200	.1	.25	1.3	15

MISCELLANEOUS ITEMS

FOOD	Measure or Weight	Food Energy Cal.	Proteins Gms.	Carbohydrates Gms.	Fat Gms.	Cholesterol Mg.	Calcium Mg.	Iron Mg.	Sodium Mg.	Vitamin A IU.	Thiamin Mg.	Riboflavin Mg.	Niacin Mg.	Vitamin C Mg.
Minestrone (USDA)	1 cup	105	5	14	3		37	1		2350	.07	.05	1	—
Minestrone (Campbell)	10 oz.	110	5	15	3		4%	2%	1075	35%	4%	2%	4%	★
Split pea (USDA)	1 cup	145	9	21	3		29	1.5		440	.25	.15	1.5	1
Split pea with ham (Campbell)	10 oz.	210	10	30	5		2%	8%	905	8%	8%	4%	6%	2%
Tomato (USDA)	1 cup	90	2	16	3		15	.7		1000	.05	.05	1.2	12
Tomato (Campbell)	10 oz.	110	2	20	2		★	4%	1050	10%	4%	2%	6%	45%
Tomato made with milk (Campbell)	10 oz.	210	7	27	7		15%	4%	1125	15%	6%	15%	10%	45%
Vegetable beef (USDA)	1 cup	80	5	10	2		12	.7		2700	.05	.05	1	—
Vegetable beef (Campbell)	10 oz.	90	6	10	3		★	4%	1135	20%	2%	2%	4%	4%
Vegetarian (USDA)	1 cup	80	2	13	2		20	1		2940	.05	.05	1	—
Vegetarian vegetable (Campbell)	10 oz.	90	2	16	2		2%	4%	820	30%	4%	2%	4%	2%

FOOD	Measure or Weight	Food Energy Cal.	Proteins Gms.	Carbo-hydrates Gms.	Fat Gms.	Choles-terol Mg.	Calcium Mg.	Iron Mg.	Sodium Mg.	Vitamin A IU.	Thiamin Mg.	Ribo-flavin Mg.	Niacin C Mg.	Vitamin C Mg.
— Canned, Ready to Serve														
Chunky beef (Campbell)	9½ oz.	210	15	21	7		2%	15%	1145	50%	4%	6%	10%	8%
Chunky chicken (Campbell)	9½ oz.	200	14	20	7		2%	8%	1075	20%	6%	10%	20%	★
Chunky vegetable (Campbell)	9½ oz.	140	3	22	4		6%	6%	1280	50%	4%	2%	6%	8%
— Dehydrated, Prepared														
Bouillon cubes, approx. ½ in. (USDA)	1 cube	5	1	Trace	Trace		—	—		—	—	—	—	—
Chicken noodle with meat (Lipton)	1 cup	70	3	9	2		★	2%		★	★	2%	6%	★
Chicken rice (Lipton)	1 cup	60	3	8	2		★	2%		★	★	★	2%	★
Noodle soup (Lipton)	1 cup	50	2	7	2		★	2%		★	★	2%	2%	★
Onion soup (Lipton)	1 cup	35	1	6	1		2%	2%		★	★	2%	2%	★
Tomato vegetable (Lipton)	1 cup	70	2	12	2		★	2%		★	★	2%	4%	★

MISCELLANEOUS ITEMS

FOOD	Measure or Weight	Food Energy Cal.	Proteins Gms.	Carbo-hydrates Gms.	Fat Gms.	Choles-terol Mg.	Calcium Mg.	Iron Mg.	Sodium Mg.	Vitamin A IU.	Thiamin Mg.	Ribo-flavin Mg.	Niacin C Mg.	Vitamin C Mg.
Vegetable beef (Lipton)	1 cup	60	3	8	1		2%	2%		★	★	2%	2%	★
SPREADS AND SAUCES														
Barbecue sauce (USDA)	1 cup	230	4	20	17		53	2		900	.03	.03	.8	13
Sandwich spread (Bennett's)	1 tbsp.	45	0	4	3				140					
Sandwich spread (Hellmann's Best Foods)	1 tbsp.	60	0	2	46		★	★	195	★	★	★	★	★
Tarter sauce (USDA)	1 tbsp.	75	Trace	1	8	5	3	.1		30	Trace	Trace	Trace	Trace
Tarter sauce (Bennett's)	1 tbsp.	80	0	1	8				105					
Tarter sauce (Hellmann's)	1 tbsp.	70	0	0	8	5	★	★	180	★	★	★	★	★
White sauce, medium (USDA)	1 cup	405	10	22	31		288	.5		1150	.1	.43	.5	2
YEAST														
Yeast, active, dry (Fleischmann)	1 pkg.	20	2.8	2.9	.1				5					

FOOD	Measure or Weight	Food Energy Cal.	Proteins Gms.	Carbo-hydrates Gms.	Fat Gms.	Choles-terol Mg.	Calcium Mg.	Iron Mg.	Sodium Mg.	Vitamin A IU.	Thiamin Mg.	Ribo-flavin Mg.	Niacin C Mg.	Vitamin C Mg.
Yeast, active, cake (Fleischmann)	1 cake	20	2.7	1.9	.1				3					
Yeast, baker's dry active (USDA)	1 pkg.	20	3	3	Trace		3	1.1		Trace	.16	.38	2.6	Trace
Yeast, brewer's, dry (USDA)	1 tbsp.	25	3	3	Trace		17	1.4		Trace	1.25	.34	3	Trace

RECOMMENDED DAILY DIETARY ALLOWANCES,[a] Revised 1974

	Age (years)	Weight (kg) (lbs)		Height (cm) (in)		Energy (kcal)[b]	Protein (g)	Fat-Soluble Vitamins				
								Vitamin A Activity (RE)[c] (IU)		Vitamin D (IU)	Vitamin E Activity[e] (IU)	Ascorbic Acid (mg)
Infants	0.0-0.5	6	14	60	24	kg×117	kg×2.2	420[d]	1,400	400	4	35
	0.5-1.0	9	20	71	28	kg×108	kg×2.0	400	2,000	400	5	35
Children	1-3	13	28	86	34	1300	23	400	2,000	400	7	40
	4-6	20	44	110	44	1800	30	500	2,500	400	9	40
	7-10	30	66	135	54	2400	36	700	3,300	400	10	40
Males	11-14	44	97	158	63	2800	44	1,000	5,000	400	12	45
	15-18	61	134	172	69	3000	54	1,000	5,000	400	15	45
	19-22	67	147	172	69	3000	54	1,000	5,000	400	15	45
	23-50	70	154	172	69	2700	56	1,000	5,000		15	45
	51+	70	154	172	69	2400	56	1,000	5,000		15	45
Females	11-14	44	97	155	62	2400	44	800	4,000	400	12	45
	15-18	54	119	162	65	2100	48	800	4,000	400	12	45
	19-22	58	128	162	65	2100	46	800	4,000	400	12	45
	23-50	58	128	162	65	2000	46	800	4,000		12	45
	51+	58	128	162	65	1800	46	800	4,000		12	45
Pregnant						+300	+30	1,000	5,000	400	15	60
Lactating						+500	+20	1,200	6,000	400	15	80

FOOD AND NUTRITION BOARD, NATIONAL ACADEMY OF SCIENCES–NATIONAL RESEARCH COUNCIL

	Water-Soluble Vitamins						Minerals					
	Folacin[f] (µg)	Niacin[g] (mg)	Riboflavin (B₂) (mg)	Thiamin (B₁) (mg)	Vitamin B (mg)	Vitamin B₁₂ (µg)	Calcium (mg)	Phosphorus (mg)	Iodine (µg)	Iron (mg)	Magnesium (mg)	Zinc (mg)
Infants	50	5	0.4	0.3	0.3	0.3	360	240	35	10	60	3
	50	8	0.6	0.5	0.4	0.3	540	400	45	15	70	5
Children	100	9	0.8	0.7	0.6	1.0	800	800	60	15	150	10
	200	12	1.1	0.9	0.9	1.5	800	800	80	10	200	10
	300	16	1.2	1.2	1.2	2.0	800	800	110	10	250	10
Males	400	18	1.5	1.4	1.6	3.0	1200	1200	130	18	350	15
	400	20	1.8	1.5	2.0	3.0	1200	1200	150	18	400	15
	400	20	1.8	1.5	2.0	3.0	800	800	140	10	350	15
	400	18	1.6	1.4	2.0	3.0	800	800	130	10	350	15
	400	16	1.5	1.2	2.0	3.0	800	800	110	10	350	15
Females	400	16	1.3	1.2	1.6	3.0	1200	1200	115	18	300	15
	400	14	1.4	1.1	2.0	3.0	1200	1200	115	18	300	15
	400	14	1.4	1.1	2.0	3.0	800	800	100	18	300	15
	400	13	1.2	1.0	2.0	3.0	800	800	100	18	300	15
	400	12	1.1	1.0	2.0	3.0	800	800	80	10	300	15
Pregnant	800	+2	+0.3	+0.3	2.5	4.0	1200	1200	125	18[h]	450	20
Lactating	600	+4	+0.5	+0.3	2.5	4.0	1200	1200	150	18	450	25

See footnotes on page 252.

ᵃ The allowances are intended to provide for individual variations among most normal persons as they live in the United States under usual environmental stresses. Diets should be based on a variety of common foods in order to provide other nutrients for which human requirements have been less well defined. *

ᵇ Kilojoules (kj) = 4.2 × kcal

ᶜ Retinol equivalents

ᵈ Assumed to be all as retinol in milk during the first six months of life. All subsequent intakes are assumed to be half as retinol and half as β-carotene when calculated from international units. As retinol equivalents, three fourths are as retinol and one fourth as β-carotene.

ᵉ Total vitamin E activity, estimated to be 80 percent as α-tocopherol and 20 percent other tocopherols.

ᶠ The folacin allowances refer to dietary sources as determined by *Lactobacillus casei* assay. Pure forms of folacin may be effective in doses less than one fourth of the recommended dietary allowance.

ᵍ Although allowances are expressed as niacin, it is recognized that on the average 1 mg of niacin is derived from each 60 mg of dietary tryptophan.

ʰ This increased requirement cannot be met by ordinary diets; therefore, the use of supplemental iron is recommended.

* National Research Council, Food and Nutrition Board, 1974. *Recommended Dietary Allowances,* 8th rev. ed. Washington, D.C., National Academy of Sciences.

Courtesy National Dairy Council U.S.A.

Footnotes

[1] Value applies to unfortified product; value for fortified low-density product would be 1500 I.U. and the fortified high-density product would be 2290 I.U.

[2] Contributed largely from beta-carotene used for coloring.

[3] Outer layer of fat on the cut was removed to within approximately ½ inch of the lean. Deposits of fat within the cut were not removed.

[4] If bones are discarded, value will be greatly reduced.

[5] Measure and weight apply to entire vegetable or fruit including parts not usually eaten.

[6] Based on yellow varieties; white varieties contain only a trace of cryptozanthin and carotenes, the pigments in corn that have biological activity.

[7] Year-round average. Samples marketed from November through May, average 20 milligrams per 200-gram tomato; from June through October, around 52 milligrams.

[8] This is the amount from the fruit. Additional ascorbic acid may be added by the manufacturer. Refer to the label for this information.

[9] Value for varieites with orange-colored flesh; values for varieties with green flesh would be about 540 I.U.

[10] Value listed is based on products with label stating 30 milligrams per 6 fl. oz. serving.

[11] For white-fleshed varieties value is about 20 I.U. per cup; for red-fleshed varieties, 1,080 I.U. per cup.

[12] Present only if added by the manufacturer. Refer to the label for this information.

[13] Based on yellow-fleshed varieties; for white-fleshed varieties value is about 50 I.U. for 114-gram peach and 80 I.U. per cup of sliced peaches.

[14] This value includes ascorbic acid added by manufacturer.

[15] Values for iron, thiamin, riboflavin, and niacin per pound of unenriched white bread would be as follows:

	Iron Mg.	Thiamin Mg.	Riboflavin Mg.	Niacin Mg.
Soft crumb	3.2	.31	.39	5.0
Firm crumb	3.2	.32	.59	4.1

[16] Unenriched cake flour used unless otherwise specified.

[17] This value is based on product made from yellow varieties of corn; white varieties contain only a trace.

[18] Based on product made with enriched flour.

[19] Iron, thiamin, riboflavin, and niacin are based on the minimum levels of enrichment specified in standards of identity promulgated under the Federal Food, Drug and Cosmetic Act.

[20] Iron, thiamin, and niacin are based on the minimum levels of enrichment specified in standards of identity promulgated under the Federal Food, Drug, and Cosmetic Act.

[21] Year-round average.

[22] Based on the average vitamin A content of fortified margarine. Federal specifications for fortified margarine require a minimum of 15,000 I.U. of vitamin A per pound.

Food Companies Listed in Nutrition Book

General Mills
Proctor and Gamble
Banquet Foods Corporation
RJR Foods
Best Foods
Breakstone Sugar Creek Foods
Buitoni Foods Corporation
Campbell Soup Company
Contadina Foods, Inc.
Del Monte
Derby Foods, Inc.
Doxsee Food Corporation
General Foods
Gerber Company
Hershey Food Company
Hunt-Wesson Foods, Inc.
ITT Continental Baking Co., Inc.
Kellogg Company
Libby, McNeill & Libby
Thomas J. Lipton, Inc.
Morningstar Farms (Miles Laboratories)
Mrs. Paul's Kitchens, Inc.
Oscar Mayer
Nabisco
Ocean Spray Cranberries, Inc.
Pillsbury
Quaker Oats, Company
S & W Foods, Inc.
Standard Brands, Inc.
Sunshine Biscuits, Inc.
Uncle Ben's Foods
Wm. Underwood Co.
Green Giant Company
Beatrice Foods Co.